THE NO NONSENSE ATTACHMENT THEORY WORKBOOK

JEFFREY C. CHAPMAN

Disclaimer

The contents of this book, including the exercises, techniques, and insights provided, are intended for educational and self-help purposes only. The author of this book is not a licensed mental health professional, medical practitioner, or therapist, and the information presented should not be construed as professional medical or psychological advice.

The strategies and suggestions found within these pages are based on the author's personal experience, research, and general understanding of anxious attachment and related subjects. They are not meant to diagnose, treat, or cure any medical or mental health condition.

Readers who are dealing with mental health challenges or who have specific concerns related to anxious attachment or any other emotional or psychological issues are strongly encouraged to seek the guidance of qualified mental health professionals.

The author and publisher have made every effort to ensure the accuracy and completeness of the information contained in this book but assume no responsibility for errors, inaccuracies, omissions, or any inconsistency herein. The reader assumes all risks and responsibilities for their use of the materials and information within this book.

Please consult with a healthcare provider if you need professional assistance with any health-related or mental health concerns.

CONTENTS

CHAPTER ONE

A COMPREHENSIVE GUIDE TO ATTACHMENT STYLES

So, you're at a party, and there's music, people talking, and laughs. The three months you've spent dating Alex have gone swimmingly, or so you thought. You look around the room and spot Alex engaged in discussion with another person. Your heart races, your palms start to sweat, and a torrent of ideas flash through your head without warning: "Is Alex more keen on that individual? To what extent does this affect us? Where do you suggest I go? Should I give them some room?

It's like being on an emotional rollercoaster without paying for a ticket. What if, however, you learned the reasoning behind your emotions? What if you could foresee these emotional reactions, guide yourself through them, or even rewire them?

Enter Attachment Theory. A psychological framework that clarifies your social interactions, your comfort with closeness and autonomy, and the motivations behind your responses to these situations. Attachment theory isn't just useful for understanding romantic or sexual relationships; it can also explain your relationships with friends, family, and even your barista. What's even better? It's not fixed; with self-awareness and effort, you can develop a more stable approach to relating to other people.

In this chapter, we'll investigate attachment in great detail. We'll go over the characteristics of the four most common types so you can determine which best describes you: Secure,

Anxious, Avoidant, and Disorganized/Fearful-Avoidant. Let's warn those up and down feelings: we've got exploring to do.

• • • ● • ● • ● • • •

The Birth of Attachment Theory

John Bowlby, was a mid-twentieth-century British psychiatrist fascinated by the emotional bonds between mothers and children, laid the groundwork for what we now call Attachment Theory[1]. He observed both idyllic and painful moments, such as tearful farewells at daycare centers, and pondered the source of this emotional push and pull.

Mary Ainsworth, an American-Canadian psychologist, was similarly enthralled by these emotional bonds. Together Bowlby and Ainsworth decided to test these theories in the laboratory. She conducted a series of research titled "Strange Situation"[2]. Ainsworth discovered that children had distinct attachment styles in response to being separated from and then reunited with their mothers.

This dynamic duo, Bowlby and Ainsworth, gave us a ground-breaking framework for understanding the invisible emotional threads that bind us together. They provided us with the vocabulary to explain why we feel secure, anxious, possessive, or distant in our relationships. And voila, Attachment Theory was born, revolutionizing how psychologists, scientists, and even common people like us understand human connection.

• • • ● • ● • ● • • •

The Four Pillars of Attachment Styles

So now you know the story of how John Bowlby and Mary Ainsworth entered the unknown world of emotional bonds. What are these attachment styles that they so brilliantly exposed?

Secure Attachment

The gold standard, Secure Attachment, should be our first step. People with this style are like emotional gymnasts; they balance their own needs with those of others with the grace of Simone Biles on the balance beam. They're okay with being close, but they also respect their partners' need for privacy and space. Securely attached people typically had a stable and loving childhood. They are the ones who trust easily but not blindly and go into relationships with an open mind and heart.

Anxious Attachment (a.k.a. Preoccupied)

People frequently compare anxious attachers to someone holding a bouquet of red flags. But it's not all bad news. They are incredibly sensitive to the needs of their partner, sometimes to the exclusion of their own. People who are anxious attachers frequently worry about being left alone. They may be called "clingy" or "needy," but what they really want is emotional closeness and reassurance.

Avoidant Attachment (a.k.a. Dismissive)

Now let's talk about the Avoidant types. They are the loners in the attachment world. Nearly as much as they detest emotional confrontations, they enjoy their own space. Avoidant people often appear independent and self-sufficient, but deep down, they want to connect with others just as much as anyone else. They've just built a wall around their feelings. Think of them as the porcupines of the emotional animal kingdom. You can get close to them, but only if you know how to deal with their quills.

Disorganized Attachment (a.k.a. Fearful- Avoidant)

Last but not least, we have the Disorganized or Fearful-Avoidant attachers. These people can change their emotional state at any time, showing signs of both anxious attachment and avoidant attachment depending on their mood or the situation they are in. Often, this unstable emotional state is caused by traumatic experiences in the past or inconsistent caregiving experiences. They want to be close to each other but are very afraid of getting hurt, which causes them to constantly be in an emotional tug-of-war.

$$\cdot \; \cdot \; \cdot \; \bullet \cdot \bullet \; \cdot \; \bullet \; \cdot \; \cdot \; \cdot$$

Your Personal Attachment Style: A Mirror to Your Emotional World

"All these attachment styles are fascinating, but how do I know which one is me?" you may ask. Well, you're in luck. We're about to go on an introspective journey, sort of like emotional spelunking. After all, this is a workbook, so let's do some work. Put on your "helmet and flashlight" because it's time to explore the caves of your emotional landscape.

The Reflective Exercise

Before we start with a structured questionnaire, let's do a reflective exercise. Consider your most recent or important relationship. How did you feel when you weren't with this person? Were you worried, calm, uninterested, or a fluctuating combination of these? Think about how you responded in arguments, when you were apart, and even in everyday situations. There's no need to rush; take your time and write down what you think. As we go deeper, this will serve as your emotional starting point.

The Questionnaire

Let's get a little more methodical now. You'll find a thorough questionnaire in chapter 4 that will help you identify your primary and maybe secondary attachment styles. These questions will look into different parts of your emotional responses, social interactions, and even your gut feelings in different situations. Don't worry; there are no right or wrong answers; only keys to a better understanding of yourself.

The Points System

After you've filled out the questionnaire, you'll add up your answers using a simple scoring system. This will put you into one of the four main attachment styles, or it may show that you have traits of more than one. Remember, though, that this isn't a magazine personality test; it's a tool for self-awareness and growth.

· • • • • • • • • • ·

Why It's Not Just a Box You Fit Into

You've determined your attachment style, and now you're wondering, "Is this my emotional fate?"

Not so fast.

While attachment styles provide a useful framework for understanding how you relate to others, they are not permanent stamps on your emotional passport.

Consider your attachment style to be a dialect, not a set language. Your attachment style can change based on experiences, self-awareness, and yes, even therapy, just as someone from New York might pick up a southern drawl after years in Texas.

Attachment Styles: Their Flexibility

You should learn the phrase "earned security" to better understand how you feel emotionally. You might begin with an anxious or avoidant attachment style, but you can "earn" a secure attachment style through conscious effort, healthy relationships, and sometimes professional guidance.

The Role of Therapy

Don't undervalue the importance of a good therapist on this journey. Cognitive Behavioral Therapy (CBT), for example, has been shown to be effective in helping people change their attachment style to one that is more secure. Professional assistance can make all the difference if you're struggling with ingrained attachment issues, especially those stemming from traumatic events or early childhood experiences.

To Recap

So, what have we found during this emotional archaeological dig? Thanks to John Bowlby and Mary Ainsworth, we now know where Attachment Theory came from. We've talked about the four main attachment styles—Secure, Anxious, Avoidant, and Disorganized/Fearful-Avoidant—that shape how we connect with others. Remember, though, that these styles aren't set in stone but rather flexible states of being that can change over time with work and maybe some professional assistance.

You may be dying to know: What's the science behind all of this now that you've had a taste of this potent framework. How are these attachment styles shaped by our brains, hormones, and even our pasts? Hold onto your curiosity, because that's exactly where we're going next. Attachment Theory is more than just sitting back and thinking about psychology; in Chapter 2, you'll learn about the neurological and psychological bases that support it.

Prepare to learn more about attachment style, where science and the soul converge.

---

1. Bowlby, J. "Attachment and Loss: Volume 1: Attachment," 1969, Basic Books

2. Ainsworth, M.D.S.; Bell, S.M. "Attachment, Exploration, and Separation: Illustrated by the Behavior of One-Year-Olds in a Strange Situation," Child Development, 1970

CHAPTER TWO

THE SCIENCE OF ATTACHMENT—IT'S NOT JUST FOR GEEKS

Imagine being given a toolbox full of gadgets and gizmos. You're told that these tools can help you have better relationships and even fix ones that are broken. The only problem is that you have no idea what these tools are for or how to use them. You could wing it, sure, but wouldn't it be better to know the nuts and bolts—literally—of how these tools work?

That's where attachment science comes in. Understanding the biological, psychological, and even hormonal aspects of attachment isn't just something academics or neuroscience buffs do. Anyone who wants to improve their emotional intelligence needs to know this. It's like learning how a car works before you drive it. You don't have to be a certified mechanic to know what's going on under the hood, but it can make the ride smoother and help you get around when things get rough.

• • • • ● • ● • ● • • •

The Brain and Attachment: Your Emotional Command Center

Imagine your brain as the master conductor of your emotional orchestra. It's not just a spongey mass in your skull; it's an incredibly advanced command center. And when it comes to attachment, two areas of the brain are particularly important: the amygdala and the prefrontal cortex.

The Amygdala: Your Emotional Alarm System

Let's start with the amygdala, an almond-shaped cluster of cells deep within your brain. Think of it as your emotional security system, constantly on the lookout for threats and rewards. Your amygdala lights up like a Christmas tree when you feel a strong emotional connection or danger in a relationship. Your amygdala is responsible for gut reactions such as feeling instantly at ease with someone or sensing something is wrong.

The Prefrontal Cortex: The Rational Counterpart

Now let's talk about the prefrontal cortex, which is located directly behind your brow. If the amygdala is the impulsive teenager of your brain, the prefrontal cortex is the wise elder. It teaches you to think before acting, analyze situations, and weigh the pros and cons. Your prefrontal cortex is doing the heavy lifting when you're deciding whether to bring up a sensitive topic with your partner or how much emotional space to give them.

The Dynamic Duo

These two parts of the brain cooperate. The amygdala may sound the alarm, but the prefrontal cortex decides whether the situation is imaginary or if something needs to be done. According to studies, people with secure attachment styles typically have a better connection between these two parts of the brain[1].

You now have a brief overview of how your brain affects your attachment style without all the boring scientific terms. Different parts of your brain work together to shape how you form emotional bonds, respond to relationship stressors, and make choices in your love life.

Hormones and Emotions: Your Body's Favorite Mixology

So, we've talked about the brain's role in attachment, but what about the hormones that run through your body? Yes, love—and attachment—might be a chemical cocktail, but we love it.

Oxytocin: The Love Hormone

Oxytocin, also known as the "love hormone" or "cuddle hormone," is the star of the show. Your body produces oxytocin when you hug someone you care about, share a private moment, or even breastfeed a baby. This hormone makes you feel warm and fuzzy inside and strengthens your bonds with others. It's like the bartender who makes the ideal Old Fashioned; it just makes everything better.

Cortisol: The Stress Messenger

Cortisol, the "stress hormone," is on the other end of the spectrum. Cortisol levels rise when a relationship is rocky or when you feel insecure. It's like that shot of tequila you didn't really need; it wakes you up but can make things a little unstable. Cortisol levels that are too high can make it harder for you to form secure attachments, which can make you feel more anxious or avoidant.

The Balancing Act

Like any good cocktail, it's all about the balance. How safe or anxious you feel in your relationships is influenced by the constant dance between oxytocin and cortisol. You have a healthy attachment when the balance is right. When it's off, though, you might feel anxious, avoidant, or disorganized in your attachment style.

The Chemical Symphony

It's not just these two hormones, of course. Dopamine, serotonin, and a host of other biochemicals join the party, each of which contributes to the complicated emotional states we experience in relationships. However, learning about the main roles that oxytocin and cortisol play can help you understand how you attach to others.

• • • ● • ● • ● • • •

Evidence-Based Research: The Proof Is in the Emotional Pudding

Longitudinal Studies: The Minnesota Longitudinal Study of Risk and Adaptation

One of the most groundbreaking studies in this field is the Minnesota Longitudinal Study of Risk and Adaptation, led by researchers Byron Egeland and Alan Sroufe. This study began in the 1970s and has followed individuals from infancy to adulthood. What's remarkable is that the study discovered a consistent link between early attachment styles and later-life outcomes like academic success, emotional well-being, and even marital stability. It's similar to a crystal ball, but it's supported by rigorous science[2].

Cross-Cultural Relevance: van IJzendoorn and Kroonenberg's Meta-Analysis

Marinus H. van IJzendoorn and Pieter M. Kroonenberg conducted a meta-analysis of attachment styles across cultures and discovered something astounding. While the prevalence of attachment styles varied by culture, the basic architecture of Secure, Anxious, and Avoidant attachments remained consistent. This was a game changer because it effectively disproved attachment theory's Western origins and demonstrated its universal applicability[3].

Therapy and Treatment: Emotionally Focused Therapy (EFT)

Emotionally Focused Therapy (EFT), developed by Dr. Sue Johnson, is a type of couples therapy that has been empirically proven to be effective in assisting individuals in transitioning from insecure to secure attachment styles. The therapy focuses on creating and strengthening emotional bonds between partners and has been particularly effective in treating relationship distress. EFT has been empirically tested for more than 20 years and has been found to be effective in 70-75% of cases[4].

The Workplace and Beyond: Attachment in Organizational Psychology

Researchers in organizational psychology, such as Mikulincer and Shaver, have investigated how attachment styles affect work relationships. Their research shows that secure attachments improve team collaboration and leadership effectiveness. On the other hand, avoidant or anxious attachments can contribute to workplace conflicts and inefficiencies[5].

The Role of Genetics: Nature's Blueprint or Nurture's Handiwork?

When you identify your attachment style, you might wonder, "Did I inherit this? Is it in my DNA?" It's tempting to believe that our attachment styles are predetermined by our genes, but the truth is a little more nuanced. We are shaped by the interaction of genetics and environment—nature and nurture.

Twin Studies: Double Trouble or Double Insight?

Twin studies have helped shed light on the genetic aspects of attachment. For instance, identical twins were more likely than fraternal twins to have similar attachment styles, according to a study by Avinun and Knafo. This genetic similarity, however, only accounted for about 35% of the variance in attachment styles[6].

Beyond Genetics: The Environmental Factor

Let us not undervalue the importance of the environment. The same twin study mentioned above leaves about 65% of the variance unexplained by genetics, implying a significant impact from environmental factors. This could range from parenting styles to life events that influence attachment behaviors, such as trauma or significant relationships.

The Chicken or The Egg: Why It Doesn't Really Matter

While it's tempting to get caught up in the "which came first" debate, it's not very productive. The important takeaway is that attachment styles are malleable, regardless of whether genetics or environment play a larger role. Because of your genes or early life experiences, you are not doomed to a life of anxious or avoidant attachment.

So, whether you're Team Nature or Team Nurture, you're a product of both. Understanding this can help you make conscious choices that can improve your attachment style.

To Recap

We've ventured through the intricacies of the brain, delved into the hormonal cocktail that influences our attachments, scrutinized the validity of this theory through well-cited research, and even questioned the role of genetics. But why? Why should you care about the amygdala, cortisol, or twin studies?

Because understanding the science behind attachment isn't just a mental exercise or trivia to impress your friends at dinner parties. It's a pathway to self-discovery and transformation. When you understand the mechanics—be they neurological, hormonal, or genetic—you gain the tools to tinker, adjust, and improve.

It's like finally understanding the rules of a game you've been playing your entire life. Once you know how it works, you can play it better. You can make informed decisions, anticipate emotional reactions, and navigate relationships with a newfound sense of agency. And that, dear reader, is the power of understanding the science behind attachment. It's not just information; it's transformation.

· · ● · ● · ● ● · ·

Want to Learn More?

Books

1. "Attached: The New Science of Adult Attachment and How It Can Help You Find – and Keep – Love" by Amir Levine and Rachel Heller

2. "The Brain That Changes Itself: Stories of Personal Triumph from the Frontiers of Brain Science" by Norman Doidge

3. "Hold Me Tight: Seven Conversations for a Lifetime of Love" by Dr. Sue Johnson

4. "Wired for Love: How Understanding Your Partner's Brain and Attachment Style Can Help You Defuse Conflict and Build a Secure Relationship" by Stan Tatkin

5. "Insecure in Love: How Anxious Attachment Can Make You Feel Jealous, Needy, and Worried and What You Can Do About It" by Leslie Becker-Phelps

6. "Born Together—Reared Apart: The Landmark Minnesota Twin Study" by

Nancy L. Segal — This book provides a comprehensive overview of the Minnesota Twin Study, offering insights into how genetics and environment shape us.

7. "Why Zebras Don't Get Ulcers" by Robert M. Sapolsky — For readers interested in the hormonal aspects like cortisol and stress, this book is an accessible dive into how our bodies react to stressors.

8. "The Developing Genome: An Introduction to Behavioral Epigenetics" by David S. Moore — This book is a fantastic resource for those interested in the intersection of genetics and environment.

Online Resources

1. The Attachment Project: attachmentproject.com

2. Psychology Today's section on Attachment: psychologytoday.com

3. The Greater Good Science Center at UC Berkeley, covering various psychology topics including attachment: greatergood.berkeley.edu

4. The International Attachment Network (IAN): ian-attachment.org.uk

5. Twins Early Development Study (TEDS): teds.ac.uk — An ongoing British study that examines the genetic and environmental contributions to psychological development.

6. Hormones.org: hormones.org — A comprehensive resource for understanding the role of hormones in human behavior.

7. The Genomic Psychology Lab: genomicpsychlab.org — Run by Dr. Robert Krueger, this lab focuses on understanding how genetic and environmental factors contribute to the development of psychological traits.

These resources offer a range of perspectives, from academic to practical, on attachment theory and its scientific underpinnings. Whether you're a novice or someone looking to deepen your understanding, there's something here for everyone.

---

1. Coan, J.A., Schaefer, H.S., & Davidson, R.J. "Lending a Hand: Social Regulation of the Neural Response to Threat," Psychological Science, 2006

2. Egeland, B., & Sroufe, L. A. "Attachment and early maltreatment," Child Development, 1981; Sroufe, L. A., Egeland, B., Carlson, E. A., & Collins, W. A. "The Development of the Person: The Minnesota Study of Risk and Adaptation from Birth to Adulthood," Guilford Press, 2005

3. van IJzendoorn, M.H., & Kroonenberg, P.M. "Cross-cultural patterns of attachment: A meta-analysis of the Strange Situation," Child Development, 1988

4. Johnson, S.M. "The Practice of Emotionally Focused Couple Therapy: Creating Connection," Routledge, 2004

5. Mikulincer, M., & Shaver, P.R. "An attachment perspective on leadership," Leadership and Management in Engineering, 2007

6. Avinun, R., & Knafo, A., "Parenting as a Reaction Evoked by Children's Genotype: A Meta-analysis of Children-as-Twins Studies," Personality and Social Psychology Review, 2014

CHAPTER THREE

THE ROLE OF CHILDHOOD AND PAST TRAUMA

Emily's Aha Moment

Emily sat in her therapist's office, nervously fidgeting with her necklace. "I just don't get it," she sighed. "Why do I always feel so insecure in relationships?"

Her therapist gave her a warm welcome. "Have you ever thought about how your childhood experiences may be influencing your attachment style today?"

The question hung in the air like a thick fog. Emily's thoughts returned to her childhood—her father's emotional unavailability and her mother's volatile mood swings. She had always thought of those as separate chapters in her life, stashed away like dusty photo albums in an attic. But what if those early memories were more than just old photos? What if they were more like seeds that grew into the emotional patterns she now recognized in her adult relationships?

This wasn't about assigning blame. Her parents, flawed as they were, carried their own burdens and histories. This was about understanding, about tracing the origins of her emotional blueprint. And with that understanding came the ability to change, to lay a more secure emotional foundation going forward.

To varying degrees, Emily's story could be any of ours. Our childhood experiences and past traumas frequently play an outsized role in our attachment styles, which are influenced by a variety of factors, including genetics and even hormonal balances. This chapter will investigate why this is, not as a finger-pointing exercise, but as a necessary step on the path to self-awareness and transformation.

· · · ● ● · ● ● · ·

Early Attachments: Where It All Begins

Consider the following: A six-month-old baby named Lucas reaches out his tiny arms, instinctively seeking the warmth of his mother's embrace. Lucas is already learning the fundamentals of attachment at this young age. Lucas' rapidly developing brain receives the following message when his mother picks him up and cuddles him: "The world is secure. We adore you."

Now imagine Lucas is five years old and about to begin kindergarten. He clings to his mother's leg, terrified of this new adventure. Nonetheless, with a little encouragement and a lot of love, he takes those first steps into the classroom. This represents yet another turning point in Lucas' understanding of attachment. He's learning that as long as he has a safe place to return to, it's okay to explore the world.

These are more than just heartwarming childhood memories; they are foundational experiences that shape Lucas' attachment style. The consistent love and support from his caregivers become internalized, forming what psychologists call a "secure internal working model." This model serves as his emotional GPS, guiding him as he grows in how to interact with others, manage stress, and form relationships.

In contrast, Sarah did not have the same fortune as Lucas. Her mother was preoccupied with work and personal issues, and she frequently neglected Sarah's emotional needs. Sarah was typically left alone to "cry it out." Sarah learns a different lesson as she gets older: "The world is unpredictable, and you can only rely on yourself." Sarah carries this insecure internal working model into her adult relationships, manifesting as anxious or avoidant attachment behaviors.

The emotional foundation we lay in our early years has a huge impact. Understanding these early attachments provides a valuable lens through which to view your current attachment style, whether you identify more with Lucas or Sarah or somewhere in between. It's like deciphering the emotional DNA that makes you who you are in relationships today.

• • • ● ● ● ● ● • •

Scars That Shape Us: The Trauma Connection

Jack is a charming, outgoing guy in his late 20s who appears to have it all—good looks, a steady job, and a vibrant social circle. But when it comes to relationships, Jack is like a ship at sea, unable to anchor to any port for an extended period of time. Jack, you see, carries the unhealed wounds of childhood trauma—his father was abusive, and his mother was neglectful. For Jack, intimacy is a double-edged sword; he craves it while also fearing it.

Lisa is a successful lawyer who excels at winning cases but struggles to maintain relationships. Her younger brother was killed in a car accident when she was 12 years old. The trauma shattered her family and left her with an insidious form of emotional baggage. Lisa developed an avoidant attachment style as a protective mechanism against the pain of loss.

Both Jack and Lisa are examples of how traumatic events or relationships can have a significant impact on one's attachment style. Trauma has a way of hijacking the emotional brain, making it difficult to form secure attachments. For Jack, the trauma manifests as a fear of intimacy and a pattern of sabotaging relationships. For Lisa, it manifests as emotional unavailability and a reluctance to rely on anyone.

· • • ● •● • ● • • ·

The Neuroscience of Trauma and Attachment

Understanding the relationship between trauma and attachment frequently takes us through the neurobiology of our brain. When trauma knocks on our door, especially during our formative years, it doesn't just leave a calling card; it sets up shop, influencing how our brain's neighborhoods such as the hippocampus, prefrontal cortex, and amygdala evolve over time. This can frequently result in a heightened state of alert, making the world appear dangerous, which can impede our ability to form secure and stable bonds with others.[1].

Furthermore, the dance between trauma and attachment is not over. It also includes our hormonal orchestra. Trauma can disrupt the balance of hormones such as cortisol, dubbed the "stress mailman," and oxytocin, dubbed the "cuddle courier," complicating our ability to form warm, nurturing bonds.

The story of trauma and attachment isn't about assigning blame or making excuses for relationship problems. Understanding the choreography of our neurobiological dance, acknowledging the steps shaped by previous experiences, and learning new moves to foster healthier, more secure attachments are all part of the process.

Unpacking the trauma suitcase and investigating its impact on attachment can provide a road map for better understanding our relational world. We can begin the journey toward healing by tenderly exploring the imprints left by past traumas, gradually rewriting the narrative of our interpersonal relationships and stepping into a realm of more secure attachments.

Breaking the Cycle: The Power of Awareness and Healing

Consider Michelle, a woman in her early thirties who experienced a string of failed relationships and couldn't figure out why. It wasn't until she started therapy that she realized she had an anxious attachment style, which stemmed from her turbulent relationship with her alcoholic mother. Michelle realized she had been looking for validation from her partners to compensate for the maternal love she had never fully received.

Michelle took action to break the cycle after becoming aware of it. She underwent trauma-specific therapies such as Cognitive Behavioral Therapy (CBT) and Eye Movement Desensitization and Reprocessing (EMDR). Michelle gradually noticed a shift in her approach to relationships. She felt less anxious, more secure, and, most importantly, she became more aware of her emotional triggers and how to manage them.

The Role of Therapeutic Interventions

Therapeutic interventions can be an invaluable resource in changing attachment styles for many people, including Michelle. Such therapies provide a safe environment in which to explore past traumas, comprehend their impact, and learn new ways of relating to oneself and others. Mindfulness and emotional regulation techniques, for example, can be especially beneficial in this transformative journey.

The Path to Secure Attachment is Not a Sprint.

It is critical to understand that changing one's attachment style does not happen overnight. It's a process, sometimes a long and difficult one. However, every step forward is a step away from the painful patterns of the past and toward a more secure and fulfilling future.

The amazing thing about human psychology is its adaptability. You have the power to change once you are aware of the underlying factors that contribute to your attachment style, particularly those related to past traumas. And, as they say, the only constant is change.

---

1. Cross, D., Fani, N., Powers, A., Bradley, B., (2017). Neurobiological Development in the Context of Childhood Trauma. National Library of Medicine https://www.ncbi.nlm.nih.gov/pmc/articles/

CHAPTER FOUR

SELF-ASSESSMENT: DISCOVER YOUR ATTACHMENT STYLE

Being aware of your attachment style is like having a map to help you find your way through the complicated journey of relationships. Let's look at Mark, a 30-year-old man who always ends up in relationships that don't last. He has noticed a pattern: whenever his relationships start to look like they could last, he feels uneasy and wants to pull away. It's a frustrating cycle that makes him feel alone and makes his partners confused.

For Mark, learning about his attachment style is both helpful and inspiring. When he looks at his past interactions and reactions in relationships through this lens, he can better understand them. Understanding his attachment style has given Mark a lot of useful information about himself. It's like discovering a key to a lock he wasn't aware of, letting in opportunities for growth and better relationships.

Figuring out Mark's attachment style is a big step toward solving his relationship problems, but it won't solve them right away. It shows you how to become more self-aware, which can lead to change, freedom from the things that keep you from being close, and stronger, more satisfying relationships. Mark has a solid base for building healthier relationships thanks to the simple act of self-evaluation. He can now slowly steer his relationship ship toward calmer waters.

• • • ● ● • ● • ● • •

Attachment Style Self-Assessment Questionnaire

Disclaimer:

Note: The following questionnaire is intended for reflective and educational purposes only. It is not a scientifically validated test and should not be used as a substitute for professional advice. For a more accurate understanding of your attachment style, consult a qualified mental health professional.

Instructions:

For each statement below, rate how much you agree or disagree on a scale of 1 to 5, where 1 stands for "Strongly Disagree" and 5 stands for "Strongly Agree."

Questions

1. **When I'm alone, I feel a sense of unease.**
   1 - Strongly Disagree
   2 - Disagree
   3 - Neutral
   4 - Agree
   5 - Strongly Agree

2. **Emotional intimacy is something I usually avoid.**
   1 - Strongly Disagree
   2 - Disagree
   3 - Neutral
   4 - Agree
   5 - Strongly Agree

3. **My fear of abandonment tends to affect my relationships.**

1 - Strongly Disagree

2 - Disagree

3 - Neutral

4 - Agree

5 - Strongly Agree

4. **Independence is less important to me than having a close relationship.**

1 - Strongly Disagree

2 - Disagree

3 - Neutral

4 - Agree

5 - Strongly Agree

5. **I often feel others are not as invested in our relationship as I am.**

1 - Strongly Disagree

2 - Disagree

3 - Neutral

4 - Agree

5 - Strongly Agree

6. **I am wary of depending too much on other people.**

1 - Strongly Disagree

2 - Disagree

3 - Neutral

4 - Agree

5 - Strongly Agree

7. **Others often describe me as "too clingy" or "needy."**

1 - Strongly Disagree

2 - Disagree

3 - Neutral

4 - Agree

5 - Strongly Agree

8. **Being vulnerable with someone is a comfortable experience for me.**

1 - Strongly Disagree

2 - Disagree

3 - Neutral

4 - Agree

5 - Strongly Agree

9. **I am concerned that people will take advantage of me if I get too close.**

1 - Strongly Disagree

2 - Disagree

3 - Neutral

4 - Agree

5 - Strongly Agree

10. **I seek advice and comfort from friends or family when I'm distressed.**

1 - Strongly Disagree

2 - Disagree

3 - Neutral

4 - Agree

5 - Strongly Agree

11. **I find it hard to rely on others because I think they might let me down.**

1 - Strongly Disagree

2 - Disagree

3 - Neutral

4 - Agree

5 - Strongly Agree

12. **The thought of my partner leaving me makes me anxious.**

1 - Strongly Disagree

2 - Disagree

3 - Neutral

4 - Agree

5 - Strongly Agree

13. **I enjoy my freedom and prefer not to make long-term commitments.**

1 - Strongly Disagree

2 - Disagree

3 - Neutral

4 - Agree

5 - Strongly Agree

14. I often find myself giving more than I receive in relationships.

1 - Strongly Disagree

2 - Disagree

3 - Neutral

4 - Agree

5 - Strongly Agree

15. Opening up to others is difficult for me.

1 - Strongly Disagree

2 - Disagree

3 - Neutral

4 - Agree

5 - Strongly Agree

16. I feel comfortable when someone I care about is also independent.

1 - Strongly Disagree

2 - Disagree

3 - Neutral

4 - Agree

5 - Strongly Agree

17. I worry that being too emotional will drive people away.

1 - Strongly Disagree

2 - Disagree

3 - Neutral

4 - Agree

5 - Strongly Agree

18. I get uncomfortable if someone wants to be very close.

1 - Strongly Disagree

2 - Disagree

3 - Neutral

4 - Agree

5 - Strongly Agree

19. **My partner's approval is extremely important to me.**

1 - Strongly Disagree

2 - Disagree

3 - Neutral

4 - Agree

5 - Strongly Agree

20. **I try to solve my problems independently rather than asking for help.**

1 - Strongly Disagree

2 - Disagree

3 - Neutral

4 - Agree

5 - Strongly Agree

• • • ● ● • ● ● • •

Scoring Guidelines:

1. Add up your scores for questions 1, 3, 5, 7, 12, 14, 17, 19.

   ○ **This gives you an "Anxious Attachment" score.**

2. Add up your scores for questions 2, 6, 9, 11, 13, 15, 18, 20.

   ○ **This gives you an "Avoidant Attachment" score.**

3. Add up your scores for questions 4, 8, 10, 16.

   ○ **This gives you a "Secure Attachment" score.**

Interpretation:

- **Higher "Anxious Attachment" score:** Indicates you may tend to seek closeness and be more concerned about your relationships.

- **Higher "Avoidant Attachment" score:** Suggests you might maintain emotional distance and value your independence.

- **Higher "Secure Attachment" score:** Reflects a balanced approach to relationships, feeling comfortable with intimacy and independence.

Disclaimer:

Note: The scores from this questionnaire are not diagnostic and should not replace professional advice. For a deeper understanding of your attachment style, please consult a qualified mental health professional.

What Your Score Means

The score you've obtained from this questionnaire isn't a definitive label but a tool for better understanding of your relational dynamics. It's a window into recognizing patterns that might have been invisible to you before. Here's a more detailed insight into what your scores might suggest:

Secure Attachment (Score Range: 4-20)

- **Very Secure (17-20):** You're more secure than Fort Knox when it comes to relationships—comfortable both in your own skin and in letting others in.

- **Secure (13-16):** You're like the cushion on a good office chair—mostly supportive, with just the right give and take.

- **Moderately Secure (9-12):** You've got a couple of emotional pebbles in your shoe, but nothing you can't handle with a bit of self-awareness.

- **Low Security (4-8):** You're in the shallow end of the emotional pool, but consider this an invitation to wade deeper into understanding and improving your relationships.

Anxious Attachment (Score Range: 8-40)

- **Very Anxious (33-40):** Your internal relationship weather forecast often calls for scattered emotional showers.

- **Anxious (25-32):** You have some rain clouds of anxiety, but also intervals of clear skies. Knowing is half the battle.

- **Moderately Anxious (17-24):** Your emotional atmosphere is mostly sunny with a chance of occasional drizzles.

- **Low Anxiety (8-16):** You're like the emotional desert—mostly dry, but don't ignore the occasional cloud.

Avoidant Attachment (Score Range: 8-40)

- **Very Avoidant (33-40):** You're not just guarding your emotional treasure; you've got it locked in a vault.

- **Avoidant (25-32):** You've got a bit of an emotional moat, but you've also left the drawbridge down here and there.

- **Moderately Avoidant (17-24):** Your emotional landscape includes some fences but also some open fields.

- **Low Avoidance (8-16):** You're more of an emotional picnic area than a fortress—accessible but with some boundaries.

This self-assessment is the first thing you need to do to learn about attachment theory. You can use the scores as a starting point to learn more about yourself and grow as a person by getting an idea of how you tend to form attachments. The goal is not to label, but to bring out patterns. Also, keep in mind that attachment styles can change over time with self-awareness, work, and sometimes help from a professional. You can always grow and change. You're not stuck where you are. Your attachment style is not a death sentence; it's a way for you to learn about yourself and get better.

Congratulations on finishing the first part of this journey of self-reflection. The questionnaire gave you a lot of information about yourself that was like being given a map to a place you had never been before. It's a bright beginning to a journey that could lead to growth, understanding, and better relationships.

You'll find that this newfound knowledge helps you move forward in the next chapters. Attachment theory will continue to grow, giving you not only new ideas but also real ways to improve your attachment style. Whether you agreed with the secure, anxious, or avoidant tendencies, there is a way for you to grow and change.

The chapters that follow are full of exercises, real-life examples, and expert advice that will help you on this journey. As you turn each page, you'll get closer to a safer and more satisfying way of interacting with other people. Your attachment style is not a fixed trait; it is a living, changing part of you.

As this chapter comes to a close, think about what you've learned about yourself. Keep your open mind and curiosity as you get ready to learn more. The road ahead looks bright and is full of chances to grow, not only in understanding your attachment style but also in building relationships that are meaningful and satisfying.

You are just getting started on your journey to improve your attachment style. The chapters that are yet to come will help you with this deep personal journey. Are you ready to go? Let us turn the page.

CHAPTER FIVE

PARENTING AND ATTACHMENT: AN OVERVIEW

Jeanne was sitting at home on a warm afternoon when her three-year-old son, Timmy, threw crayons around, laughed, and was full of energy. Just like Timmy's bright drawings that were on the fridge, life was a happy mix of colors. Jeanne's life was full of interesting things, but she often found herself traveling through time to think about her childhood.

As Jeanne was growing up, her home had strict rules and serious faces. She thought her parents were good, but they were a bit too far away, like the strong oak trees in their backyard. Talking about feelings was as rare as rain in the desert, and hugs were only given on birthdays.

Jeanne wanted to give her son a different picture when she became a mother. She wanted to paint a picture with open conversations, warm hugs, and a sky where feelings could float freely. But there were some problems along the way. The ghost of her past would sometimes come back to haunt her present, making her withdraw into herself for a short time, especially when she was stressed.

Jeanne was reading a book about parenting one day when she came across a chapter on attachment theory. It was like someone had given her a mirror that showed not only herself but also the parenting styles of the generations that came before and after her. It made sense of how her parents' attachment styles had, in a way, painted her own attachment picture.

That changed when she had Timmy. She was determined to paint a picture of strong attachment on it. Understanding attachment theory helped her find her way through the complicated paths of parenting. It was a way to break the cycle and make sure that her relationship with her son was as warm and comforting as the sun in the evening.

Through Jeanne journey of reflection, we see how parenting has a huge effect on attachment. As we go through this chapter, we'll look at how different parenting styles can shape a child's attachment style. From the tight grip of authoritarian parenting to the soft embrace of authoritative parenting, each style changes a child's emotions in a way that can't be erased.

Thus, let's start this journey of discovery by looking into how parenting and attachment are connected and how understanding this connection can help build safe and fulfilling relationships between parents and children.

• • • ● • ● • • •

Parenting Styles and Their Impact

As the first few months of parenting go by, parents often find themselves at a crossroads, trying to decide which way they want to go as parents. The decisions that parents make at this point often have a big effect on how they bond with their children in the future. How the parents raise their children has a big impact on the type of bond that forms, whether it's secure or not.

Authoritative parenting:

Parents who are authoritative are like a strong bridge between being strict and loving. They make clear rules, but they are also caring and responsive. It seems like they have one foot in the ground of discipline and the other in the water of empathy. Kids who grow up with parents who are in charge often feel safe, heard, and valued. They are likely to develop a secure attachment style because they know that when life gets rough, they can just call their safe harbor for comfort.

Authoritarian Parenting:

To understand what authoritarian parenting is all about, picture a fortress with high walls and strict rules. These parents put discipline and obedience above all else, which makes it hard for kids to talk to their parents. Their love is strong, but the way they show it might get lost in the rigidity. When kids grow up with this kind of parenting, they may often be in the middle of anxious attachment, where they want to be accepted, or avoidant attachment, where they learn to be independent to protect themselves from the cold winds of emotional unavailability.

Permissive parenting:

They are like a soft breeze that doesn't say "no" very often. There aren't clear lines between things, and giving in is normal. It's like a playground without any fences. Kids are free to play and explore, but they might want a safe boundary that tells them they are safe here. The type of attachment that forms could go back and forth between anxious and avoidant. Children may become anxious when they are looking for or avoiding structure. They may learn to navigate life's playground on their own early on, missing out on the comforting embrace of secure attachment.

Neglectful Parenting:

Parents who don't care about their kids or aren't involved are like a barren land where emotional support is hard to come by. Children are lost in a wilderness of insecurities when they don't get enough attention, care, or rules. When parents do these things, their kids' attachment styles are often all over the place. Kids can get wrapped up in fear, the need for love, and mistrust if they don't get consistent care.

No matter what parenting style you employ, it will influence your child's attachment style. The interactions the child had as a child will influence their future relationships. This understanding is beautiful because it can show parents how to make changes that will help them build a secure attachment with their kids. We can always change the way we parent and steer our child toward the safe shores of secure attachment, where the sun of emotional availability shines brightly and the seed of trust and love between parent and child grows.

· · · ● · ● · ● · · ·

Earned Security

In the field of attachment theory, the phrase "earned security" is like a candle of hope. Foreshadowing the message that the story of attachment is not set in stone, but can be changed with awareness and hard work. Earned security is about moving from an insecure attachment to a secure one, both for yourself and as a way to leave a legacy of love and trust for your children.

Let's look into the life of Emily, a young mother who grew up in a home where feelings were like fleeting shadows that were hard to see and rarely acknowledged. For her, the realm of secure attachment was like a language she had never heard before. As she held her baby, she was determined that the first language her child would learn would be the language of love and safe attachment.

It's kind of like learning this new language of attachment to feel safe. It's about unlearning the habits you picked up as a child and learning how to make safe, caring connections again. Emily had to think about herself, understand herself, and make a conscious effort to meet her child's needs in a way that was caring and dependable.

The most important thing about earned security is that it can change things. Parents can build secure attachments with their kids, even if they have had trouble with attachments in the past. The change not only affects the way the parent attaches to others, but it also sets the stage for the child to experience the world through the lens of secure attachment.

To become secure, people often have to look into their pasts, figure out how their parents' attachment styles affected them, and try to fill in the gaps through hard work, education, and sometimes therapeutic intervention. It's like taking care of a garden: you have to fix up the soil, plant new seeds, and then love, wait, and be consistent with them so that the secure attachment flowers can grow and cover the whole garden of the parent-child relationship.

Earned security is a concept that shows how caring parenting has a big effect on the fabric of attachment. It's an invitation for parents to step into the realm of possibility, to change the rules of attachment, and to leave their children and grandchildren a legacy of love, trust, and safe attachment.

· · · ● · ● · ● · · ·

Strategies for Change

Starting to work on fostering secure attachment is like going into a garden; you'll need to care for it and watch as strong bonds form between you and your children. It is a journey filled with understanding, patience, and a variety of doable strategies that can help you reach the sunny realms of secure attachment.

Cultivate Emotional Availability:

Your child needs you to be there for them emotionally, just like the sun shines on the garden. As long as you are there for your child, both physically and emotionally, you are like a roof over their head.

Engage in Reflective Parenting:

Being a reflective parent is like holding a gentle mirror to your actions, feelings, and reactions. To understand the feelings that are swirling beneath the surface, you need to stop and think about how you interact with your child. You can learn more about your child's and your own feelings by reflecting on your own parenting.

Practice Responsive Parenting:

Pay attention to your child's wants, needs, and feelings, just like a river changes its course as it flows. Being aware of and meeting your child's needs at the right time and in the right way builds trust and a strong bond with them.

Encourage Open Communication:

Set the mood so that words can flow freely like a gentle stream. Help your child talk about their feelings, fears, and happiness. By listening well, you build trust with your child and let them know that you value what they have to say.

Learn the Language of Love:

For each child, love comes in different forms, such as words of affirmation, quality time, touch, acts of service, or gifts. Find out what your child's love language is and use it. It's like singing a sweet lullaby to your child, which strengthens your bond with them.

Seek Support and Education:

Building secure attachment is a journey where you keep learning new things. Get help from parenting groups in your area, educational materials, or a professional. Being willing to learn and ask for help is like having a compass and someone to go with you on this journey.

Practice Patience and Forgiveness:

There will be times when you trip up on your way to building secure attachment. You should be patient with yourself as well as your child. Let go of the mistakes and see them as steps toward a better connection and understanding.

Mindful Stress Management:

Stressful storms can temporarily obscure the views of safe attachment. Managing your stress in a mindful way by meditating, doing breathing exercises, or finding hobbies that make you feel good will keep the clouds of stress from hiding the warmth of secure attachment.

To Recap

We've learned about the profound effects of parenting on the delicate fabric of attachment by following the paths in this chapter. It's as if the gentle hands of a potter shape the clay of attachment, giving it shape, texture, and the appearance of long-lasting bonds. Every time we speak to, look at, or touch our children, we are adding a note to the symphony of attachment that can be heard in their soft heartbeats.

It's not an easy journey from the shores of insecurity to the realms of secure attachment. Being on this journey means going through waves of self-reflection, storms of old insecurities, and gentle breezes of understanding that help you sail toward the horizon of change. Good news: the compass of earned security can find its way through rough seas and land on the calm shores of secure attachment.

It's within each parent's power to change the story of attachment, to break the cycle of unstable attachments, and to leave their children a legacy of love, trust, and strong bonds. When change seeds are planted with love, understanding, and hard work, they can grow into a garden full of blooming secure attachments that paint the skies of future generations with shades of trust, love, and emotional stability.

Workbook Section: Painting the Picture of Secure Attachment

1. Reflections:

Reflect on Jeanne's journey and how her understanding of attachment theory helped her in her parenting journey.

- In what ways do you relate to Jeanne's experience?

- How has your understanding of attachment theory evolved over time?

- What steps have you taken or plan to take to improve the attachment with your child?

2. Identifying Your Parenting Style:

Based on the description of parenting styles provided, identify the style(s) that resonate most with your approach.

- What aspects of your parenting style are beneficial for fostering secure attachment?

- What changes might you consider to enhance a secure attachment?

3. Activity: Engaging in Reflective Parenting

Choose a day to practice reflective parenting. Pay close attention to your interactions with your child, and jot down your observations:

- How did your child respond to your reflective approach?

- What did you learn about your child's feelings and needs?

- What did you learn about your own reactions and feelings?

4. Exercise: Practicing Responsive Parenting

Create a scenario where you practice responsive parenting. For instance, when your child is upset or needs attention, respond promptly and appropriately. Record the scenario and outcomes:

- Describe the situation:

- How did you respond?

- What was your child's reaction?

5. Planning Ahead: Cultivating Earned Security

List three specific actions you plan to take to foster earned security in your attachment with your child.

1.

2.

3.

6. Group Discussion or Journal Prompt:

Join a parenting discussion group or reflect in your journal.

- Share your experiences and challenges in fostering secure attachment.

- Discuss the concept of earned security and how it resonates with your parenting journey.

- Share strategies and resources that have been beneficial in nurturing a secure attachment.

CHAPTER SIX

PARENTING THE SECURELY ATTACHED CHILD

Picture this: it's a bright and early Saturday morning in a busy park. Happy children's voices echo around the playground as they run and play. Among them is 6-year-old Chloe, a free-spirit whose eyes twinkle with curiosity and softly assure her of love. She runs around the playground like a young gazelle, her shrill laughter echoing off the trees. Her mother sits on a bench nearby, reading a book but remaining ever vigilant as her daughter conquers the playground's swing set, slide, and seesaw.

Chloe dashes back to her mom with a beaming smile on her face after she successfully navigates a piece of playground equipment. Chloe's mother is her rock of confidence, always there to give a bear hug, a high five, or a kind word of praise whenever Chloe experiences happiness. Chloe is able to go out into the world with the confidence that she will always return to the bench to a warm embrace of love, understanding, and reassurance from her parents.

This scene depicts a well-attached youngster. Chloe's secure attachment demonstrates itself in her fearlessness in trying new things while also reflecting her innate need to seek reassurance and affection from her mother. The mother-daughter duo of emotional availability and independence promotion provided fertile ground for the development of her secure attachment style.

Chloe and her mom are the embodiment of secure attachment in the field of psychology, which is characterized by a fine balance between love and freedom and the knowledge that no matter how large the playground of life becomes, the bench of emotional connection, understanding, and love will always be there.

· · · ● · ● · ● · · ·

Characteristics of Secure Attachment in Children

Secure attachment in children manifests through a variety of behaviors and traits that are often easily observable. Here are some key characteristics of securely attached children, which are based on their comfort and trust in their caregivers:

1. **Exploration and Curiosity**: Children who are securely attached feel safe exploring their surroundings. They have a natural curiosity and will venture out to discover new things, knowing that they can return to a safe base if necessary.[1]

2. **Social Competence**: They have stronger social skills and find it easier to make new friends. Their secure attachment lays the groundwork for comprehending and navigating social interactions.

3. **Emotional Regulation**: These kids are better at controlling their emotions. Because they have experienced responsive caregiving, they can cope with stress and recover from distress more effectively.

4. **Seeking Comfort**: When they are upset, children who are securely attached will go to their caretakers to feel better. They believe that the people taking care of them will give them the support and comfort they need.

5. **Positive Self-Esteem**: A positive self-image grows from a secure attachment. Kids feel understood and valued, which is good for their self-esteem.

6. **Open Communication**: They are more likely to be honest and open with their caregivers about their needs, feelings, and worries.

7. **Responsive to Caregiving**: Children who are securely attached respond well to caregiving, and this positive interaction strengthens the bond between the child and caregiver.

8. **Adaptability**: Because they have a strong sense of trust and safety, they can handle new situations and challenges with calm emotions.

For kids to develop these traits, the caring environment they get from caregivers who are consistent, understanding, and emotionally available is very important. In order to build secure attachment, there are many moments that teach children to trust, understand, and feel safe. These feelings affect their social, emotional, and mental health.

Fostering Security

To help a child form a secure attachment, you need to make sure they are in a safe, loving, and valued environment. Here are some activities and ideas to help your child behave well and strengthen your relationship with them:

1. **Consistent Response**:

   - Respond promptly and consistently to your child's needs and problems. The child will trust you more and know that they can count on you for help.

2. **Reflective Listening**:

   - As a way to practice reflective listening, repeat what your child says and show that you understand. You could tell your child, "It sounds like you're really upset about losing your toy," if they are upset.

3. **Emotional Validation**:

   - Don't brush off your child's feelings; instead, acknowledge them. Don't tell them not to feel a certain way. Instead, say something like, "I know that made you sad."

4. **Quality Time**:

   - Do fun things with your child to spend quality time with them. Whether you're reading, playing a game, or going for a walk together, these times can make your relationship stronger.

5. **Encouragement**:

- Help your child become independent by letting them explore and try new things. Give them praise and good things for their efforts and accomplishments.

6. **Express Love and Affection**:

- Regularly show love and affection. Being close to a child and telling them "I love you" or giving them a hug can help them feel safe.

7. **Routine and Predictability**:

- Your child will know what to expect if you stick to a routine. This feeling of knowing what will happen can give them comfort and security.

8. **Open Communication**:

- Talking to your child about their day, their worries, and their joys will help them feel more comfortable talking to you. Tell them they can talk to you about anything.

9. **Mindful Parenting**:

- Being present, patient, and aware of your child's needs and feelings are all ways to practice mindfulness as a parent.

10. **Educational Play**:

- Take part in games that are both fun and good for you. It could be puzzles, drawing, building blocks, or anything else that keeps their mind active and lets them interact with others.

11. **Parental Self-Regulation**:

- Improve how you handle your own feelings. Being a parent can be stressful, and it's important to keep your emotions in check so you can be a good role model for your child.

12. **Seek Support**:

- If you need to, don't be afraid to get help from family, friends, or professionals to deal with parenting problems.

Taking each of these steps can be a brick in building a secure attachment foundation that will give your child a safe, loving place to grow. By doing these things, you're not only building a healthy attachment, but you're also giving your child the emotional tools they'll use as adults.

· • • ● • ● • • ·

The Role of Boundaries

Setting healthy limits is a very important part of promoting secure attachment, especially between parents and children. It's about finding the right balance between being there and making someone feel safe, while also letting them be free and independent. People, especially parents and children, move back and forth between being close and far away in relationships. This is what makes secure attachments possible. There are two main ways that people can cross boundaries: by being too close or too far away. A balanced approach that values both space and proximity can help people feel safe while also encouraging their independence. [2].

Setting healthy boundaries makes it clear what is and isn't okay, which helps people respect and understand each other. Parents pretty much set the stage for secure attachments by setting and sticking to healthy boundaries. This means being clear about your limits, needs, and expectations in the relationship. This builds trust and safety, which are essential for secure attachment to grow.[3].

Setting limits gives kids a structure they can count on, especially when you're a parent. It makes a child less anxious by making their life more predictable. One way this is shown is through set rules and routines, such as times for meals, bed, homework, and other things. When parents set and enforce these rules instead of the child negotiating them, it makes the home a stable place where kids feel safe. These set boundaries make things less uncertain, which is a step toward building a secure attachment.[4]

Research shows that a parenting style that is authoritative and combines warmth with firmness when setting rules works very well. This mix not only helps kids feel safe, but it also helps parents and kids have a good relationship. A balanced approach like this one builds a secure attachment that is good for both the child's emotional health and the family as a whole.[5].

Basically, setting healthy boundaries doesn't mean being rigid or overly strict. It means making sure that kids feel safe, understood, and ultimately, securely attached. This balanced way of setting limits is one of the building blocks for a healthy attachment style, which can have positive effects on a child for a long time.

As parents start this rewarding journey, each step they take to build a secure attachment paves the way for a healthy environment where their child can grow emotionally, socially, and psychologically. Setting healthy limits, being emotionally available, and building trust and a sense of safety are all things that parents do today that are investments in their child's emotional health. Understanding and following the rules of secure attachment is a step toward building a loving and supportive relationship between a parent and child that not only strengthens the bond between the two but also sets a strong foundation for the child's future relationships. It's an ongoing journey full of chances to learn, grow, and connect deeply with others.

Even though being a parent has its ups and downs, parents should know that working to encourage these good behaviors and secure attachment is a big, rewarding job that will have a big effect on their child's emotional growth. Being there for your child, loving them no matter what, and giving them a safe place to be are all signs of love that will last their whole lives. These things will also help them develop the emotional skills they need to make lasting relationships.

• • • ● • ● • • •

Workbook Section: Nurturing Secure Attachment

1. Reflections:

Reflect on the narrative about Chloe and her mom in the park.

- How do you see your own parenting style reflected in this story?

- How does your child respond to new experiences or challenges?

- What steps can you take to be more emotionally available for your child?

2. Identifying Secure Attachment Traits:

Based on the characteristics of securely attached children outlined, rate how often you observe the following behaviors in your child on a scale of 1 to 5 (1 being never, 5 being always).

- Exploration and Curiosity: _____

- Social Competence: _____

- Emotional Regulation: _____

- Seeking Comfort: _____

- Positive Self-Esteem: _____

- Open Communication: _____

- Responsive to Caregiving: _____

- Adaptability: _____

3. Activity: Reflective Listening Practice

Choose a time to sit down with your child and ask about their day. Practice reflective listening by repeating back what they say in your own words and asking open-ended follow-up questions. Jot down your observations:

- What did you learn from your child?

- How did your child respond to this style of communication?

- How did it feel to engage in reflective listening?

4. Exercise: Setting Boundaries

Think of a recent situation where setting a boundary was necessary for the well-being of your child or your family.

- Describe the situation

- What boundary did you set?

- How was the boundary communicated and enforced?

- How did it affect the relationship and the emotional environment?

5. Planning Ahead: Fostering Security

List three specific actions you plan to take in the upcoming week to foster a secure attachment with your child. Consider aspects like spending quality time, setting clear boundaries, and practicing mindful parenting.

1.

2.

3.

6. Group Discussion or Journal Prompt:

Consider joining a parenting group or discussion forum to share experiences and learn from others. Alternatively, reflect in your journal:

- How have your attachment style and parenting practices evolved over time?

- Share a success story where nurturing secure attachment led to a positive outcome.

- What challenges do you face in nurturing a secure attachment, and how do you plan to address them?

---

1. https://www.ncbi.nlm.nih.gov/books/NBK356196/

2. https://www.attachmentproject.com/blog/
boundaries-and-attachment-styles/

3. https://www.psychologytoday.com/us/blog/
the-angry-therapist/202307/nurturing-secure-
attachment-building-healthy-relationships

4. https://www.mindbodygreen.com/
articles/healthy-boundaries-in-parenting

5. https://www.gov.uk/government/news/
helping-parents-to-parent

CHAPTER SEVEN

PARENTING THE ANXIOUSLY ATTACHED CHILD

Picture what the Thompson family does on a normal Friday night. At sunset, Joanna is cooking a hearty meal for her family. There is the delicious smell of lasagna in the air, but there is also the sound of worried cries coming from inside the house, over the clinking of dishes and the sizzle of garlic bread in the oven.

Emma, Joanna's six-year-old daughter, is fearing her shadows again upstairs. As the day turns to night, her fears grow, casting long, scary shadows on the walls of her bedroom. Even though Joanna put a happy-night light in Emma's room to keep the darkness away, her anxiety makes everyday things look like scary images.

As Joanna goes upstairs, her heart hurts with a mix of love and helplessness. She leaves the pot on low heat. Emma is huddled under the covers, and her little body shakes with every sound she thinks she hears in the dark. Joanna gives Emma a warm, comforting hug and tells her that she's safe and that mommy is right here. Emma's little heart is filled with fear, and no amount of comforting seems to calm it down.

Emma clings to Sarah with a grip that speaks volumes of her anxious attachment. Because the world is unpredictable, Emma finds it scary, so she runs to be close to her mother for safety. Her mother, who makes her feel safe, is the rock in her stormy world.

Joanna knows this is a strong love, though. A love filled with worry, neediness, and the need to be reassured all the time. The love between Joanna and Emma keeps her alert and ready to rush to Emma's side at the first sign of trouble.

Joanna knows she has a huge job to do because she is gently rocking Emma and whispering comforting words to her to calm her soul. To get through the confusing world of anxious attachment, you need a lot of patience, a lot of understanding, and a lot of love that doesn't depend on anything. As Emma stops crying and her grip on Joanna gets looser, she is reminded that the road ahead may be long and winding, but love will lead them through the storm of worry and into the calm shores of safety.

• • • ● • ● • ● ● • •

Signs of Anxious Attachment in Children

Compared to their securely attached peers, anxiously attached children frequently perceive the world as a much more dangerous and unpredictable place. The symptoms of anxious attachment in children can manifest in a variety of behaviors and patterns, which can paint a vivid picture of internal turmoil and external distress. Here is a look at some of these behaviors driven by fear and insecurity:

1. **Separation Anxiety and Inconsolability**: A child's reaction to being separated from and then reunited with their caregivers is one of the most obvious signs of anxious attachment. When the caregiver leaves, the child is in a lot of pain, and when they come back, the child may still be unable to calm down. They may be stuck in a cycle of wanting comfort but being afraid of being abandoned.[1] .

2. **Fear of Abandonment and Lack of Trust**: Because the child can't get over the fear of being left alone, despite the caregiver's assurances, this fear leads to a general mistrust of the caregiver's reliability.[2] .

3. **Poor Emotional Regulation**: Children who are anxiously attached frequently have trouble controlling their feelings. They might have trouble naming their

emotions and have trouble controlling their emotions.[3].

4. **Difficulty with Peer Relationships**: For children who are anxiously attached, making and keeping friends can be difficult. Poor relationships with other kids may result from their fear of being abandoned and trust issues, which may spread to their peers.[4].

5. **Clinginess and Limited Exploration**: To children who are anxiously attached, the outside world might seem like an unknown place full of dangers. They tend to cling to their parents and other caregivers, looking for safety in the known and avoiding exploring their surroundings.[5]

6. **Generalized Anxiety**: A general anxious demeanor is common, and it can show up as a fear of strangers, intense emotional pain, or a desire to avoid being alone. They may also show signs of codependency and have trouble setting boundaries because they are afraid of being abandoned.[6]

Anxious attachment is a story about a young heart longing for safety and consistency in the midst of a swirl of fears and insecurities. Early recognition of these signs can help you understand and meet the emotional needs of anxiously attached kids, which will help them build healthier relationships as they learn how to interact with others.

· · · ● ● ● ● ● · ·

Strategies for Alleviating Anxiety

Alleviating anxiety in kids takes patience, understanding, and the right strategies. Here are some exercises, activities, and tips for navigating the maze of anxious attachment:

1. **Establishing a Predictable Routine**: Predictability is comforting to children with anxious attachment. A sense of safety and security can be created by creating a daily routine where the child knows what to expect.

2. **Practicing Mindfulness and Relaxation Techniques**: It can be beneficial to teach kids mindfulness exercises like guided imagery and deep breathing. These

techniques can give them tools to deal with their anxiety.

3. **Gradual Desensitization**: Exposing a child to certain things or situations gradually and safely can help them get used to the things or situations that make them anxious.

4. **Validating Emotions**: It's important to validate the child's feelings and fears, no matter how silly they seem. Validating their feelings allows for open communication and demonstrates that you understand their pain.

5. **Secure Base Scripting**: This strategy involves writing a story that reinforces the caregiver's availability and responsiveness. Let's consider a real-life example:

Emma, a seven-year-old with anxious tendencies, often gets nervous about school. Her mother notices this and decides to create a story for her. The story goes: "Once upon a time, Emma felt a little scared about a big math test she had at school. She told her mom about it, and her mom said, 'I'll be thinking of you, Emma. Remember, after school, we'll sit together, have some warm cookies, and you can tell me all about it. I'm always here for you.' Emma went to school, remembering her mom's words, and felt a little bit braver."

The story reinforces to Emma that her mother is consistently available, emotionally supportive, and will be there when she returns from school. By regularly sharing such stories, children are reassured of their caregiver's presence and reliability, even when they're not physically together. This can be a comforting tool, allowing them to face challenges with more confidence.

6. **Play Therapy**: Children can talk about their worries and fears in a safe and supportive environment by participating in therapeutic play.

7. **Parental Self-Regulation**: Children often mimic their parents' emotional states, so parents should also work on controlling their own emotions. A stable environment for the child can be created by practicing calmness and consistency in responses.

8. **Professional Guidance**: If the child's anxiety gets in the way of their daily life, it may be helpful to talk to a therapist who specializes in child anxiety and

attachment issues.

9. **Educational Support**: It can also be very important for the child's emotional growth if the school setting is one that is understanding and supportive of their anxious tendencies.

10. **Encouraging Social Interactions**: Over time, gently encouraging the child to make friends and interact with others can help them feel more confident and less anxious.

11. **Positive Reinforcement**: Rewarding good behavior and accomplishments, no matter how small, can help a child feel better about themselves and calm down.

12. **Attachment-Focused Parenting**: A sense of security can be fostered by adopting an attachment-focused parenting style that emphasizes being sensitive to a child's needs.

These strategies aren't quick fixes; instead, they're about creating a safe space where the child can explore the world around them, despite their anxious tendencies. Parents can assist their anxiously attached child on a path to better emotional regulation and healthier attachments by using a balanced approach of understanding, patience, and professional support when needed.

· · · ● · ● · ● · ·

Emotional Availability

"Emotional availability" in parenting refers to a parent's capacity to meet their child's deepest emotional needs, connect with them on an emotional level, and offer the support and comfort they require when they need it. This aspect of parenting is very important for a child's behavior, ability to learn, and ability to control their emotions. It involves being aware of and present with what a child is going through, taking the time to understand their worries, and addressing their issues while coming up with solutions together.[7]

When a child shows signs of anxious attachment, being emotionally available as a parent is especially important. A child with anxious tendencies frequently seeks reassurance and needs to know that their parent is there for them both physically and emotionally. A parent who is emotionally available is dependable and consistent in how they meet their child's emotional needs.

Being responsive to a child's anxiety is one aspect of being emotionally available. According to a study cited by the National Institutes of Health (NIH), parents who are supportive can help their children feel less anxious. The study showed that teaching parents how to deal with their child's anxiety may help ease symptoms. This shows how important parental responsiveness is in managing childhood anxiety.[8]

The quality of emotional exchanges between a parent and child is at the core of emotional availability. It encompasses their reciprocal accessibility to each other and their ability to understand and respond appropriately to each other's communicative signals[9]. A child with anxious attachment can benefit greatly from this kind of emotional exchange by feeling understood, safe, and supported.

Urie Bronfenbrenner, a well-known developmental psychologist, emphasized the significance of a child's emotional connection to an adult. Communities and professionals play a role in fostering this bond, which is essential for a child's healthy development.[10]

Emotional availability is a complicated idea, but it's essential to building a strong relationship between parents and kids. It includes support, sensitivity, warmth, and closeness, all of which are important for helping an anxiously attached child and improving their emotional health.[11]

In other words, being emotionally available doesn't mean denying or downplaying the child's anxiety; rather, it means understanding, recognizing, and working through those feelings with the child. The child feels safe expressing themselves in this environment, and they know that their parent will always be there for them.

Anxious attachment is not a sign of failure for either the child or the parents. It's a challenge, a part of the complicated emotional range of people that calls for compassion and understanding. When you find out that your child has a tendency toward anxious attachment, as a parent, you might feel a lot of different emotions at first, including worry, doubt, and even guilt. However, it's important to let go of self-judgment and any hurried attempts to "fix" the child.

Parents and kids aren't on different boats when they're navigating the sea of anxious attachment; instead, they're on the same boat together, learning how to steer through the waves. As they get to know each other's emotional rhythms and forge a strong, trusting bridge of secure attachment, each wave and storm becomes a little less terrifying and each storm a little more manageable.

This chapter explored the many facets of anxious attachment, highlighting the important golden threads of emotional accessibility, comprehension, and healthy coping mechanisms that can help overcome difficulties and create a web of safe, loving relationships.

The goal for parents is to create an environment where their children feel safe talking about their fears and know they will be met with love, understanding, and support, not to eliminate the anxiety that is at the heart of anxious attachment.

The journey of raising an anxiously attached child is a marathon, full of chances for development, comprehension, and strengthening the love between you and your child. Parents and children evolve, cultivating a garden of emotional security where the seeds of trust, understanding, and strong love can flourish and thrive with each step taken together and with each challenge faced head-on. This is done in addition to working on the "issue" of anxious attachment.

• • • • • • • • • •

Workbook Section: Navigating Anxious Attachment

1. Reflections:

Reflect on the narrative of the Thompson family, especially the emotions and behaviors exhibited by little Emma and her mother Joanna.

- In what ways do you resonate with Joanna's and Emma's experiences?

- How has your perception of anxious attachment evolved after reading their narrative?

- What insights have you gained about the emotional undercurrents of anxious attachment?

2. Identifying Anxious Attachment Traits:

Based on the description of anxious attachment traits provided, identify and reflect on any similar behaviors or emotions you have observed in children around you or in your own experiences.

- What traits of anxious attachment are most prominent in your observations?

- How do these traits manifest in the child's behavior and interactions?

- What impacts do you perceive these traits have on the child and their relationships?

3. Activity: Face The Fear:

Choose a relaxed and comfortable setting to engage in this activity with a child. Observe and jot down the emotions and behaviors exhibited during the activity.

- Describe the setting and preparations for the activity

- How did the child express their fears?

- What observations did you make regarding the child's emotional state and responses?

4. Exercise: Breathing Balloon:

Engage in the "Breathing Balloon" exercise with a child, and record the experience.

- Describe the process and the child's engagement with the exercise:

1. **Sit or Lie Down Comfortably**:

   Have the child sit comfortably or lie down in a quiet and relaxed setting.

2. **Visualization**:

   Instruct the child to close their eyes and imagine a balloon in their belly.

3. **Inhale**:

   Guide the child to take a slow, deep breath through their nose, envisioning the balloon in their belly expanding as it fills with air.

4. **Hold**:

   Once their belly is full, ask the child to hold their breath for a few seconds, maintaining the image of the full balloon.

5. **Exhale**:

   Now instruct the child to slowly exhale through their mouth, imagining the balloon in their belly deflating as the air goes out.

6. **Repeat**:

   Encourage the child to repeat this process several times, maintaining the visualization of the balloon expanding and deflating with each breath.

- **Discussion**:

   After practicing the breathing exercise, talk with the child about how they feel. Discuss the experience and the sensations they noticed during the exercise.

- What reactions or changes in emotional state did you observe?

- How did this exercise impact the interaction between you and the child?

5. Planning Ahead: Drafting a Security Schedule:

Create a draft of a daily "Security Schedule" aimed at adding predictability and fostering a sense of safety for the child.

- List the activities and routines included in the schedule

- Describe the intended benefits of this schedule for the child

- How do you plan to introduce and implement this schedule?

6. Group Discussion or Journal Prompt:

Engage in a group discussion or reflect in your journal:

- Share your reflections on the narrative of the Thompson family and the insights gained.

- Discuss the challenges and strategies in navigating anxious attachment.

- Share experiences and strategies that have been beneficial in supporting children with anxious attachment.

7. Mindful Stress Management Activity:

Practice a stress management technique such as mindfulness meditation or deep breathing for a week. Note any changes in your understanding or approach towards anxious attachment.

- Describe the stress management technique practiced

- Note observations and any changes experienced

- How has this practice influenced your understanding or approach towards anxious attachment?

8. Reflecting on Strategies for Change:

Reflect on the strategies outlined in the chapter for alleviating anxiety and fostering secure attachment.

- Which strategies resonate with you most?

- How do you plan to incorporate these strategies into your daily interactions with children?

- What steps will you take to further explore and apply the concepts of emotional availability and attachment-focused parenting?

---

1. https://www.simplypsychology.org/anxious-ambivalent-attachment.html

2. https://www.simplypsychology.org/anxious-ambivalent-attachment.html

3. https://www.choosingtherapy.com/anxious-attachment/

4. https://www.simplypsychology.org/anxious-attachment-style.html

5. https://www.simplypsychology.org/anxious-attachment-style.html

6. https://psychcentral.com/health/anxious-attachment-style-signs

7. https://www.fatherli.com/post/what-is-emotional-availability-and-why-is-it-important

8. https://www.nih.gov/news-events/nih-research-matters/supportive-parenting-can-reduce-childs-anxiety

9. https://www.sciencedirect.com/science/article/abs/pii/S1750946720300593

10. https://www.ncbi.nlm.nih.gov/pmc/articles/PMC7781063/

11. https://www.mdpi.com/1660-4601/20/1/68

CHAPTER EIGHT

PARENTING THE AVOIDANT CHILD

Seven-year-old Brian Carter, and his parents, lived in a busy city neighborhood where life seemed to be a marathon all the time. Brian was known for being independent, which made him stand out among his friends. While other kids clung to adults they knew in strange situations, Brian handled his little problems with a calm confidence that was both admirable and, at times, a little unsettling for his parents.

Friends and family frequently complimented Mr. and Mrs. Carter on how "well-adjusted" and "self-sufficient" Brian was. He was the boy who never made a scene, dealt with his disappointments quietly, and whose demeanor was frequently referred to as "mature beyond his years." The Carters, however, missed the small but meaningful requests for comfort and assurance that frequently come from kids: the unplanned hugs, the stories of everyday adventures, and the need for comfort after a small accident or a fight with a friend.

The Carters decided to break out of their routine on a sunny weekend and took Brian to the fair that had come to their town. The day was perfect, with the sky painting happy colors that matched the laughter and chatter filling the fairgrounds. The Carters were drawn to the carousel as they walked through the fair. Mrs. Carter's heart was filled with a simple, warm joy at the thought of riding the bright horses with Brian. Brian, however, politely said, "I'm fine, Mom," when asked. I'll just keep an eye out. The same thing happened at the ice cream stand, the Ferris wheel, and the clown show: Brian was happy to sit back and watch the world go by, politely declining invitations to join in the activities that seemed to bring other families closer together.

When the Carters got home at the end of the day, the car was quiet, and there was a quiet realization. Brian's independence was both a sign of his independence and a cover for his avoidant behavior. He politely declined, but it was probably more of a way for him to avoid the emotional conversations that often come with sharing experiences.

The tale of Brian and the Carters sheds light on the subtle signs of avoidant behavior in kids. These kids, who like to think they are independent, frequently avoid the emotional connections that are the basis of strong family bonds. It sets the stage for talking about the complicated problems and sweet hopes that come with raising an avoidant child.

•　•　•　●　•　●　•　●　•　•　•

Recognizing Avoidant Behaviors

Understanding a child's avoidant attachment style can be very helpful in understanding their current behavior and building healthier relationships in the long run. Children with avoidant attachment frequently show a strong need for independence and self-reliance, to the point where it may seem like they are little adults stuck in kid bodies. They often avoid getting close, as if they've put up a small but noticeable barrier around themselves. Even the desire for comfort that all children have seems to take a back seat. As you might expect, they don't turn to their parents or other adults who care for them for comfort when they're upset or in trouble. They ignore their feelings and keep going, like a treasure chest full of undiscovered gems.[1]

If you look someone in the eyes, they might turn away, avoiding the connection that happens when you make eye contact. Their attachment style is to blame, not mischief or shyness. Their trust is hard to earn; it's like a fortress that's hard to get through. It's hard for other people to understand what they're feeling or thinking because their emotions and thoughts are like a well-guarded castle.[2]

These kids use a map they drew themselves to find their way. They don't ask for help very often, even when the path gets rough. They seem to enjoy going on this journey by themselves or have trained themselves to do so. As if they were trying to maintain their independence at all costs, they might even avoid physical touch, which is a fundamental form of human connection.[3]

The response, or lack thereof, from their primary caregivers is frequently the cause of avoidant attachment. They learned to stop asking for help when their emotional pleas for assistance were ignored or turned down. They got used to the cold reality by developing emotional independence and learning to comfort themselves rather than looking for comfort from other people.[4]

In order to meet the specific needs of an avoidantly attached child, one must be aware of these signs. This opens the door for a more secure attachment to develop over time.

· · · ● · ● · ● · ● · ·

The Importance of Space

The study of space and emotional connection in relation to avoidant attachment reveals a complex interaction that is essential to comprehending the actions and requirements of a child with an avoidant attachment style. These kids frequently come across as fiercely independent, seeing their space as a safe haven where they can avoid the huge emotional wave that comes with relationships.[5]

The role of caregivers is crucial during the infant stage, when the world is full of new experiences. When babies are most vulnerable, they rely on their caregivers to take care of all of their needs. But when there isn't an emotional connection or when caregivers aren't available emotionally, babies change to survive. In order to protect themselves from the pain of unmet needs, this adaptation may take the form of a wall around their emotions, preventing emotional closeness or connection.[67]

In the life of an avoidantly attached child, space and emotional connection don't move in a straight line. Their actions and reactions to their surroundings are influenced by them.

These kids often have trouble letting other people into their emotional space because they seem to be stuck in a shell that's hard to break through.[8] They frequently view resources, including emotional resources, through a lens of scarcity, which may increase their need for emotional space.[9]

The irony is that while these kids want space and independence, people also have an innate need for emotional connection. Giving them the space they need while also fostering emotional connection requires a delicate touch. It requires a combination of patience, understanding, and strategies designed to bridge the emotional gap without overwhelming them. This delicate balance aims to gradually ease the child into a space where they can experience emotional connection without the fear or distress that goes along with it, moving them closer to a healthier attachment style.

The contrast between space and emotional connection in the context of avoidant attachment highlights the careful balance between encouraging independence and fostering emotional connection.

· • • ● · ● ● • · ·

Strategies for Engagement

It can be difficult to connect emotionally with an avoidant child. Here are some ideas for tactics:

1. **Building Trust and Dependency**:

    - Develop trust with your child. This can be done by acting consistently, keeping your word, and being there for your child when they need you. This lessens their anxiety and makes them more open to developing a close relationship with you.[10]

2. **Encouragement to Open Up Emotionally**:

    - Encourage your child to express their emotions. Make it a safe place for them to express their feelings and thoughts without worrying about being judged or getting in trouble. [11]

3. **Self-Esteem Building**:

- Help your child's self-esteem by recognizing their efforts and accomplishments, no matter how small. This can help them feel valued and safe.[12]

4. **Providing Stability and Security**:

- It is crucial to maintain a stable and safe environment. This includes keeping a routine, having clear rules, and giving people a sense of safety and predictability.[13]

5. **Feeling Loved**:

- Make your child feel loved and cared for. Spend time with them, listen to them, and show affection in a way that makes them feel good.[14]

6. **Establish Predictable Routines**:

- For kids with avoidant attachment, consistency is essential. Setting up routines that are predictable makes them feel safe and secure and can help them open up emotionally. [15]

These strategies are meant to build trust, safety, and emotional openness so that you can connect emotionally with an avoidant child without overwhelming them.

Sometimes it can feel like deciphering a code to navigate the emotional landscape of an avoidant child. Their outside may show independence and self-sufficiency, but deep down they have the same need for emotional connection as every other child. In the midst of all the emotions they find overwhelming, it's like a silent plea for understanding and a connection that comforts them.

Avoidant kids may appear to have an impenetrable shell around them, avoiding emotional contact and favoring the privacy of their own emotional safe spaces. However, this does not remove their innate need for emotional connection. It's important for their long-term health, their ability to make happy relationships, and their development as emotionally strong people.

Parents, it's important to remember that the lack of interest is not a rejection of emotional connection, but rather a fear of it. It may take a lot of patience, understanding, and gentle persistence to build a relationship with your avoidant child. Every little break through, every little hole in their emotional armor, is a step toward a stronger, more fulfilling relationship.

Your efforts to connect with your avoidant child and reassure them that the emotional world is not as scary as they think it is are investments in their future. It's a message that they, too, deserve love, understanding, and a strong emotional connection, despite their avoidant tendencies. They will find their way to the safe and comforting world of emotional security through the maze of avoidance if you are there to support and understand them at all times.

· · · ● · ● · ● · · ·

Workbook Section: Unraveling Avoidant Attachment

1. Reflections:

Reflect on the narrative of Brian Carter and his parents, delving into the subtleties of avoidant behavior exhibited by Brian.

- What aspects of Brian's behavior resonate with your experiences or observations?

- How has this narrative broadened your understanding of avoidant attachment?

- Are there moments in the narrative that prompted you to reflect on your own interactions with children?

2. Identifying Avoidant Attachment Traits:

Based on the detailed description of avoidant attachment traits provided, delve into any similar behaviors or tendencies you have observed or experienced.

- What prominent traits of avoidant attachment have you observed?

- How do these traits manifest in interactions and relationships?

- How do you believe these traits impact the emotional landscape of the child and those around them?

3. Activity: Emotional Availability Check

Engage in an activity where you assess and reflect on the emotional availability in your interactions with a child, jotting down observations and insights.

- Describe the setting and dynamics during this activity:

- How did the child respond to attempts at emotional connection?

- What did you learn about the child's comfort level with emotional expression and connection?

4. Exercise: Practice of Presence

Create a scenario where you practice being emotionally present and available for a child, noting down the scenario, responses, and outcomes.

- Describe the situation

- How did you exhibit emotional presence?

- What was the child's reaction?

5. Planning Ahead: Building Bridges

Draft a plan aimed at fostering a more secure attachment by gently navigating the avoidant tendencies.

- List specific actions you plan to take

- Describe how you aim to balance respect for the child's independence with the nurturing of emotional connection:

- How do you plan to assess and adapt your approach as you move forward?

6. Group Discussion or Journal Prompt:

Engage in a group discussion or reflect in your journal:

- Share your reflections on the narrative of Brian Carter and the insights gained about avoidant attachment.

- Discuss the complexities and nuances in fostering emotional connection with avoidantly attached children.

- Share experiences, challenges, and strategies that have been beneficial in nurturing emotional connection.

7. Mindful Engagement Activity:

Practice a mindful engagement technique such as mindful listening or reflective dialogue with a child, noting any changes in the level of emotional connection.

- Describe the mindful engagement technique practiced:

- Note observations and any changes experienced:

- How has this practice influenced your understanding or approach towards avoidant attachment?

8. Reflecting on Strategies for Engagement:

Reflect on the strategies for engagement outlined in the chapter.

- Which strategies resonate with you most?

- How do you plan to incorporate these strategies into your daily interactions?

- What additional resources or support might you seek to further your understanding and capability in nurturing emotional connection?

---

1. https://www.simplypsychology.org/avoidant-attachment-style.html

2. https://thehopefilledfamily.com/avoidant-attachment-in-children/

3. https://www.webmd.com/parenting/what-is-avoidant-attachment

4. https://www.parentingforbrain.com/avoidant-attachment/

5. https://cptsdfoundation.org/2018/10/15/the-turmoil-of-avoidant-attachment-style/

6. https://www.loewensteincounseling.com/blog/2020/10/13/8-parenting-behaviors-that-may-lead-to-avoidant-attachment-in-children

7. https://www.healthline.com/health/parenting/avoidant-attachment

8. https://thehopefilledfamily.com/avoidant
    -attachment-in-children/

9. https://cptsdfoundation.org/2018/
    10/15/the-turmoil-of-avoidant-attachment-style/

10. https://thehopefilledfamily.com/
    avoidant-attachment-in-children/

11. https://thehopefilledfamily.com/
    avoidant-attachment-in-children/

12. https://thehopefilledfamily.com
    /avoidant-attachment-in-children/

13. https://www.helpguide.org/
    articles/childhood-issues/
    attachment-issues-in-children.htm

14. https://www.helpguide.org/
    articles/childhood-issues/attachment-
    issues-in-children.htm

15. https://getgoally.com/blog/fearful-
    avoidant-attachment-style/

CHAPTER NINE

PARENTING THE DISORGANIZED/FEARFUL-AVOIDANT CHILD

Navigating the emotional world of a disorganized or fearful-avoidant child is like entering a world where the rules of engagement aren't always clear and the signals are often mixed. The longing for connection and the fear of it collide in this complex dance of closeness and distance. These kids' emotions are complicated by their past experiences, which may have made them wary or afraid of making close connections.

Their emotional reactions may seem erratic or unpredictable a lot of the time, which is a reflection of the turmoil they feel inside when they think about making attachments. It's a world where the need for love and affection is overshadowed by the fear of losing or being rejected, and where the desire for closeness battles the fear of getting too close.

The desire for a safe bond and the seeds of hope are present in the heart of a disorganized or fearful-avoidant child, even though they are covered in fear and uncertainty. The goal is to help the child slowly learn to trust and make healthy emotional connections by understanding their fears and recognizing their wants.

This chapter will go into detail about how to parent a child who has a disorganized or fearful-avoidant attachment style. It will give you ideas and tips on how to deal with the difficulties and build trust and safety.

Signs and Symptoms

The signs and symptoms of a child with a disorganized or fearful-avoidant attachment style can be very complex and varied. Here is a summary of the data I got from different places:

1. **Lack of Safety Perception**: Children with a fearful-avoidant attachment style frequently lack a sense of safety and are constantly convinced that something is wrong.[1]

2. **Poor Self-Regulation of Emotions**: They struggle with regulating their emotions effectively

3. **Difficulty Trusting Others**: Children like these may have a hard time trusting others, even their caregivers.

4. **Hypervigilance**: They are always on the lookout for danger signs, which shows that their fear and anxiety are high.

5. **Fear of Close Relationships**: Fear of close relationships is a defining characteristic of disorganized attachment, also known as fearful-avoidant attachment. These kids frequently have internal turmoil because they are unsure of how to act in relationships.[2]

6. **Attachment Figures Becoming Sources of Fear**: The attachment figure who may have abused the child or acted abusively in front of the child becomes a source of fear in disorganized attachment scenarios. This upsetting truth turns the supposed safe place into a threat that the child learns to stay away from in order to survive. However, the child frequently stays attached to this dangerous attachment figure, showing a very complicated attachment pattern. [3]

7. **Stress and Conflict**: When a child is unsure whether their parent will be a source of support or fear, disorganized attachment can cause them to feel

stressed and conflicted.[4]

8. **Childhood Trauma or Abuse**: A disorganized or fearful-avoidant attachment style can be significantly influenced by childhood abuse or trauma. In such cases, the child may perceive the parent as both a comfort and a threat at the same time, which further complicates their attachment dynamics.[5]

These symptoms and signs show how disorganized and emotionally unstable children with fearful-avoidant attachment frequently are. It is crucial for teachers and caregivers to be aware of these problems and deal with them so that children can get the help and support they need.

The Role of Past Trauma

Children with a disorganized attachment style are a result of traumatic experiences and inconsistent parenting. A disorganized attachment style is more likely to emerge when a child tries to connect with a parent who has unresolved trauma or an attachment injury. This is especially true when a child tries to bond with a parent but gets inappropriate or inconsistent responses during times of stress, fear, or need. These situations cause a whirlpool of feelings and actions that are typical of disorganized attachment.[67]

A paradox that causes the child to feel scared and confused is at the heart of this attachment style. Caretakers, who are supposed to be a source of safety and comfort, become sources of fear. The child develops a fearful-avoidant or disorganized attachment style when the caregiver's behavior changes frequently, especially when the child is upset. This dynamic highlights a deep-seated inconsistency that is likely to last into adulthood, affecting relationships and efforts to build trust.[8]

Disorganized attachment is facilitated by a particularly traumatic childhood, which is frequently characterized by fear, trauma, or an unstable and confusing relationship with the caregiver. Such a childhood situation does not support the development of a secure attachment style, but rather opens the door for a disorganized attachment style, which is marked by a lack of trust, fear, and confusion in relationships.[9]

A caretaker who is abusive is frequently involved in the most severe situations that result in a disorganized attachment style. A shocking 80% of babies who have been abused have insecure, disorganized attachment issues. In these situations, the child is stuck in a place that makes them afraid because the caretaker, who should be a source of safety, acts in ways that are unpredictable and hurtful. A disorganized attachment style is produced by the child's need to depend on this person for survival, which is a terrifying paradox.[10]

The formation of a disorganized attachment style is complicated on many levels when the role of past trauma and inconsistent parenting is examined. It's not just about healing old wounds; it's also about understanding and breaking a cycle of inconsistent and fear-inducing caregiving. This information is essential for starting the healing process and creating more stable attachments.

• • • ● • ● • ● • •

Navigating the Emotional Minefield

It takes patience, understanding, and well-thought-out strategies to help a child who is emotionally disorganized or fearful avoidant get through their problems. The objective is to provide a stable and secure emotional environment that challenges the child's preexisting narrative of fear and instability. Parents can use the following tactics:

1. **Consistent Responses**: Respond consistently to the child's needs and distress signals. Over time, this consistency can help the child change what they expect and feel safe and secure.

2. **Educate Yourself**: Learn about disorganized attachment and how trauma affects a child's emotional and behavioral responses. Understanding the causes of your child's actions can help you intervene more successfully.

3. **Therapeutic Intervention**: If you need it, get professional assistance. Insights and support in navigating this difficult path can be provided by therapists who specialize in attachment and trauma.

4. **Create Safe Spaces**: Create safe environments where the child can feel

understood and safe. The child may find comfort in a certain place in your home or in a particular routine.

5. **Practice Mindfulness and Regulation Techniques**: Incorporate mindfulness and emotion regulation techniques into your daily routine. In addition to helping the child deal with stress and build emotional connections, this also helps the parent.

6. **Open Communication**: Encourage open dialogue within the family. Allow your child to express their worries, fears, and other feelings without worrying about what other people will think.

7. **Validation**: Validate your child's emotions and experiences. This can help the child feel seen and understood, which is very important for forming a strong attachment.

8. **Seek Support**: A sense of community and shared understanding can be fostered by joining support groups or connecting with other parents going through similar problems.

9. **Maintain Patience and Understanding**: It's a journey that calls for patience, understanding, and a lot of love. Remember that healing and change are processes that take time, and enjoy the small victories along the way.

10. **Educational Interventions**: Special education services or individualized education plans (IEPs) are two examples of educational interventions that can help a child with their emotional and academic needs by giving them a structured and supportive environment.

11. **Develop Coping Strategies**: Teach your child coping mechanisms to control their feelings and responses to stress. This can be a part of a bigger plan to help people deal with their feelings and keep them under control.

These techniques are intended to give parents the tools they need to create a caring, stable, and emotionally secure space for their kids. This will help them heal and build strong attachments over time.

The path of disorganized attachment can feel like it's full of emotional landmines at times. But this hard work has the potential to bring about big changes for the child and the whole family. It requires a certain amount of perseverance, commitment, and a sincere desire to comprehend and heal the complicated wounds of the past.

This is not a solo endeavor; it is a group effort that frequently requires the help of experienced professionals. Therapists who specialize in attachment disorders and trauma can offer invaluable advice, support, and strategies that are specifically designed for your family's needs. Their advice can be very helpful in navigating the tricky emotional terrain and helping to create a caring, stable, and emotionally safe environment for your child.

Still, it's important to remember that change, while possible, is usually a slow, step-by-step process. It's a journey marked not only by difficulties but also by the numerous small victories that can be found along the way. No matter how small it may seem, every step forward is a step toward building a stronger attachment, which will lead to healthier, more satisfying relationships in the future.

So, if you find yourself navigating the complex web of attachment issues, remember that it's never too late to get help from a professional. Change is possible with the right help, advice, and lots of love and patience. Your efforts to give your child a stable and safe emotional environment can have a big impact on their capacity to form secure and healthy attachments, now and in the future.

· • • ● • ● • ● • ·

Workbook Section: Journey Through Disorganized Attachment

1. Reflections:

Reflect on the intertwined emotions of fear and longing for connection as elaborated in the chapter regarding disorganized or fearful-avoidant attachment in children.

- In what ways does the narrative inform your understanding of disorganized attachment?

- Can you identify any instances or experiences from your surroundings that resonate with the behaviors and emotions described in the narrative?

2. Identifying Disorganized Attachment Traits:

Based on the detailed elucidation of disorganized or fearful-avoidant attachment traits, delve into the behaviors that you have observed or experienced that align with these traits.

- Describe any instances where a child showcased a mixture of fear and longing for connection.

- How do you believe past traumatic experiences might have influenced these behaviors?

3. Activity: Observing Emotional Responses

Engage in a day of observing and noting down the emotional responses of a child, particularly focusing on their approach towards attachment and how they handle emotional conflicts.

- Describe the setting and dynamics during this activity:

- What did you discern regarding the child's comfort level with emotional expression and connection?

4. Exercise: Practicing Consistent Responses

Create a scenario where you practice responding consistently to a child's needs and distress signals, recording the scenario, responses, and outcomes.

- Describe the situation

- How did you exhibit consistent responses?

- What was the child's reaction?

5. Planning Ahead: Fostering Security

Draft a plan focusing on building a secure and stable emotional environment for a child with disorganized or fearful-avoidant attachment.

- List specific actions you plan to take

- Describe how you aim to challenge and alter the child's preexisting narrative of fear and instability:

- How do you plan to assess and adapt your approach as you move forward?

6. Further Reading and Exploration:

Delve deeper into understanding disorganized attachment and strategies for nurturing secure attachment with these additional resources:

- "Disorganized Attachment and Caregiving" by Judith Solomon and Carol George

- "Understanding Disorganized Attachment: Theory and Practice for Working With Children and Adults" by David Shemmings and Yvonne Shemmings

7. Group Discussion or Journal Prompt:

Engage in a group discussion or reflect in your journal:

- Share your reflections on the narrative and the insights gained about disorganized attachment.

- Discuss the complexities in fostering emotional security and stable attachment with disorganized or fearful-avoidant children.

- Share experiences, challenges, and strategies that have been beneficial in nurturing emotional connection.

8. Mindful Engagement Activity:

Practice a mindful engagement technique, such as mindful listening or reflective dialogue with a child, noting any changes in the level of emotional connection.

- Describe the mindful engagement technique practiced:

- Note observations and any changes experienced:

- How has this practice influenced your understanding or approach towards disorganized attachment?

9. Reflecting on Strategies for Navigating Emotional Minefield:

Reflect on the strategies for navigating the emotional minefield outlined in the chapter.

- Which strategies resonate with you most?

- How do you plan to incorporate these strategies into your daily interactions?

- What additional resources or support might you seek to further your understanding and capability in nurturing emotional connection?

---

1. https://www.simplypsychology.org/fearful-avoidant-attachment.html

2. https://www.simplypsychology.org/disorganized-attachment.html

3. https://www.verywellmind.com/disorganized-attachment-in-relationships-7500701

4. https://www.healthline.com/health/parenting/disorganized-attachment

5. https://www.helpguide.org/articles/childhood-issues/attachment-issues-in-children.htm

6. http://www.trauma-pages.com/a/fosha-03.php

7. https://www.healthline.com/health/parenting/disorganized-attachment

8. https://www.attachmentproject.com/blog/disorganized-attachment/

9. https://health.clevelandclinic.org/attachment-theory-and-attachment-styles/

10. https://www.parentingforbrain.com/disorganized-attachment/

CHAPTER TEN

NAVIGATING SECURE ATTACHMENT IN RELATIONSHIPS

Let's think about a couple named Rick and Melissa. They've been together for a long time. Their relationship isn't perfect, but it's strong and stable, which is something many couples wish they had

When it comes to things like who should pick up the groceries or where they should go on vacation, they do argue with each other. But here's where they really shine: in how they handle these disagreements. When they disagree, they listen to each other, don't put the other person down, and try to find a solution instead of arguing about who is right. They are honest about what they want and need without worrying about being judged or ignored. They feel safe in their relationship because they know they have each other's backs.

Over the years, they've built a relationship based on trust, understanding, and respect. This has made them feel safe with each other. It's not the kind of love that makes you feel butterflies in your stomach that movies often show. Instead, it's a stronger bond that has stood the test of time.

There are some bad things about their relationship, but it shows that a securely attached relationship is a solid base that gives each person the support and understanding they need to thrive.

• • • ● • ● • • •

Characteristics of Secure Attachment

Safe attachment means that both people in a relationship trust each other, feel comfortable with each other, and can talk to each other clearly. It means being able to relate to each other in a way that is consistent, interdependent, and full of confidence. Based on information from different sources, here are some specific traits of secure attachment in relationships:

1. **Interdependence**: It's possible for people in securely attached relationships to depend on each other while still having their own identity and independence.

2. **Consistency**: People who have secure attachments consistently interact with others in a way that makes them feel safe and supported.

3. **Effective Communication**: Secure attachment depends on being able to talk to each other well. People can talk about their wants, needs, and concerns in a way that is respectful and understanding.[12]

4. **Emotional Regulation**: Being able to control your emotions, especially when things are hard or stressful, is a sign of a secure attachment.

5. **Comfort with Emotional Intimacy**: People who are securely attached are okay with being emotionally close to others and can connect with them on a deeper level without worrying about being open.

6. **Ability to Trust**: A secure attachment is based on trust, which means that both people believe their partners are reliable and honest.

7. **Ability to Seek and Provide Support**: People who are securely attached can ask their partners for help when they need it and are also willing to give help in return.

8. **Comfort in Solitude**: People with secure attachment value their relationships,

but they are also happy to be alone and have a healthy sense of independence.

9. **Lack of Anxiety in Relationships**: People who are securely attached don't spend a lot of time or energy worrying or feeling bad about their relationships.[3]

These traits help people build long-lasting, satisfying relationships in which both people feel valued, understood, and supported.

$$\bullet \ \bullet \ \bullet \ \bullet \ \bullet \ \bullet \ \bullet \ \bullet \ \bullet \ \bullet$$

Security-Building Activities

A secure attachment isn't built through big actions or a one-time effort. It's built through small actions done regularly over time. These exercises and tips can help you build or keep secure attachment traits in your relationships, whether they're with a partner, a child, or even a friend:

1. **Active Listening**:

   ○ Active listening means showing that you are interested in and care about what other people are saying. This kind of good communication builds trust, strengthens emotional bonds, and finds healthier ways to settle disagreements.[4]

2. **Expressive Communication**:

   ○ Tell people what you want, need, and how you feel. Tell your partner they should do the same. It's important to make sure that both of you feel safe enough to say what you want without worrying about being judged.

3. **Playful Interaction** (especially for parent-child relationships):

   ○ Do things with your child like "Playful Copycat" or "mirroring the child," where you don't need any toys or other physical items. Just be there with your child and be ready to talk. This activity gets the parent and child involved and in tune with each other.[5]

4. **Routine Bonding Activities**:

- Include regular activities that bring you together in your daily life. This could be as easy as having dinner together, going for a walk, or setting aside time to "talk" about your day and any worries or feelings you may have.

5. **Understanding and Responding to Cues** (especially for parent-infant relationships):

- Understand your baby's unique cues and act on them. For example, you could pay attention to when they eat and sleep and talk, laugh, and play with your baby, building a secure attachment bond from a very young age.[6]

6. **Maintaining Physical Closeness**:

- Being close to each other physically by hugging, holding hands, or just sitting close can make you feel safe and secure in the relationship.

7. **Spend Quality Time Together**:

- Spend time with each other. Spending quality time together is important for keeping a relationship strong.

8. **Practice Patience and Understanding**:

- There are good and bad times in every relationship. Have patience, understand, and be ready to work through problems with others.

9. **Educate Yourself**:

- It can also be helpful to understand the theory behind attachment. It can be helpful to know what a secure attachment looks like and what kinds of actions and attitudes help it happen.[4].

10. **Seek Professional Help if Necessary**:

- You might find it helpful to talk to a therapist if you have trouble building a secure attachment. They can help you come up with strategies and give you support.

The goal of all of these activities and methods is to build trust, understanding, and respect, which are the most important parts of a secure attachment. Remember that the goal is to make a safe, caring, and supportive space that encourages honest communication and being emotionally available.

• • • • • • • • • •

The Role of Communication

Communication is the link that holds people together, helping them understand each other and making strong, safe bonds. Truthful and open talking is very important in relationships because it helps people feel safe and attached. Communication alone isn't enough; there needs to be a healthy level of engagement that includes understanding, empathy, and response.

When people in a relationship feel like they can say what they want without worrying about being judged or laughed at, trust and safety grow. This is especially important when there is trouble or disagreement. The essence of communication is a key part of safe attachment in the following ways:

1. **Expression of Needs and Desires**:
   People who feel safe in their relationships can talk about their wants, needs, and worries without holding back. Realizing your own emotions and experiences helps others do the same, so just being yourself is important.

2. **Emotional Availability**:
   It's important to be emotionally available for your partner or child, to be present, and to listen to how they're feeling. It's about being there, not just physically, but also mentally and emotionally, and showing that you understand and care.

3. **Conflict Resolution**:
   There will be disagreements in every relationship, but how they are handled is what makes a difference. Open communication lets people with different opinions say what they think in a healthy way and helps people come to a

solution that takes everyone's needs and feelings into account.

4. **Building Trust**:

Being honest and open with each other builds and strengthens trust. It's about being honest and dependable and making a safe space where people can be themselves.

5. **Validation**:

A deep human need is to feel heard and accepted. When people feel like their feelings and experiences are understood and accepted, it makes them feel safe and strengthens their attachment bond.

6. **Non-verbal Communication**:

Talking isn't the only way to communicate. Body language, eye contact, and touch are also nonverbal ways to show care, understanding, and assurance, which can help build a secure attachment.

7. **Feedback and Constructive Criticism**:

In a securely attached relationship, it's important to give respectful and positive constructive feedback, even when it's about problems or issues. This helps both people grow and understand each other better.

8. **Maintaining an Open Dialogue**:

Keeping the lines of communication open, even when things are hard, is what makes an attachment feel safe. It means keeping the lines of communication open and sharing your thoughts, feelings, and experiences, which makes the relationship stronger.

Communication that is clear, open, and respectful is like a tapestry that holds a secure attachment together. In a secure attachment environment, people can thrive, feel understood, and be valued. This builds a strong base for secure attachment to grow.

Getting to the place of secure attachment isn't a one-time thing; it's an ongoing process, like taking care of a garden. It needs constant care, understanding, and a willingness to change with each other as life goes through its different stages. Rick and Melissa's story shows that even in a securely attached relationship, there will be times when things don't go as planned. But it's the ability to bounce back from problems and keep talking that helps the bond stay strong and grow.

This chapter talks about different aspects of secure attachment. These aspects show how important trust, understanding, and good communication are for maintaining a securely attached relationship. Also, the exercises aren't just things to check off; they're meant to help you understand each other better and build a stronger bond, which leads to a secure attachment.

Creating a safe space where people feel seen, heard, and valued is at the heart of secure attachment. It's not a place you want to get to; it's a journey with changing dynamics that needs conscious effort, patience, and the care of a safe, respectful, and open communication channel. As you move forward in your relationships, may the ideas and activities in this chapter help you build and maintain the secure attachment that makes it possible for deep, meaningful connections.

· · · · ● · ● · ● · · ·

Workbook Section: Cultivating Secure Attachment

1. Real-World Reflection:

Reflect on the story of Rick and Melissa. Their story unfolds a tale of a relationship adorned with trust, understanding, and the art of effective communication.

- How do you relate to Rick and Melissa's story?

- Identify and jot down the elements in their relationship that resonate with the secure attachment traits discussed in the chapter.

2. Active Listening Exercise:

Engage in a dialogue with a partner or a close friend, practicing the art of active listening. Share your experiences, the challenges faced, and the insights gained.

- What did you learn about your listening skills?

- How did the conversation flow change with active listening?

3. Expressive Communication Challenge:

Choose a day to practice expressive communication with those around you. Be open about your needs, desires, and feelings. Encourage others to do the same.

- Record your experiences

- How did people react to your openness?

- What challenges did you face and how did you overcome them?

4. Routine Bonding Time:

Establish a routine bonding activity, like dinner together or a nightly walk. Reflect on the change in connection and understanding over a week.

- Describe the activity and the routine

- How has this routine impacted your relationship and communication?

5. Non-Verbal Communication Observation:

For a day, pay close attention to the non-verbal cues shared between you and your loved ones.

- Record your observations

- How did non-verbal communication contribute to the understanding and bond shared?

6. Conflict Resolution Scenario:

Create a hypothetical conflict scenario. With a partner, practice resolving it through open communication, understanding, and compromise.

- Describe the scenario

- How was the conflict resolved?

- What secure attachment traits were utilized?

7. Feedback and Constructive Criticism Exercise:

Exchange constructive feedback with a trusted individual. Reflect on the experience, the emotions felt, and the outcome of the exchange.

- How did it feel to give and receive constructive feedback?

- How can constructive criticism foster a secure attachment?

8. Validation Exercise:

Practice validation with those around you. Validate their feelings, experiences, and opinions. Note the reactions and the impact on the relationships.

- Describe your experiences

- How did validation influence the communication and bond shared?

9. Reflection on Security-Building Activities:

Reflect on the security-building activities shared in the chapter.

- Which activity resonated with you the most?

- Create a plan to incorporate these activities into your daily life to foster secure attachment.

10. Group Discussion or Journal Reflection:

Reflect on the journey towards secure attachment as depicted in the chapter. Share experiences, insights, and the practical application of the security-building activities in nurturing secure attachment.

- How have the insights from this chapter influenced your perspective on secure attachment?

- Share any personal anecdotes, challenges, or victories experienced on the journey towards fostering secure attachment.

---

1. https://psychcentral.com/health/4-attachment-styles-in-relationships

2. https://mentalhealthmatch.com/articles/relationships/secure-attachment

3. https://debbiegrammas.com/7-characteristics-of-secure-attachment/

4. https://www.psychologytoday.com/us/blog/the-angry-therapist/202307/nurturing-secure-attachment-building-healthy-relationships#

5. https://psychcentral.com/pro/child-therapist/2014/08/5-attachment-based-activities-to-strengthen-parent-child-relationships

6. https://www.helpguide.org/articles/parenting-family/building-a-secure-attachment-bond-with-your-baby.htm

CHAPTER ELEVEN

UNDERSTANDING AND IMPROVING ANXIOUS ATTACHMENT AS AN ADULT

You keep looking at your phone all afternoon, even though it's just a normal Sunday. After hanging out with friends, your partner said they'd text you when they got home. Your message has been waiting for hours. Your mind starts to spin with a lot of ideas. What if they don't like being with you as much as they like being with their friends? How about if they don't want to come home to you? Every minute that goes by makes the thoughts that maybe, just maybe, you're not as important as you thought you were stronger.

In this picture, you can see how someone with an anxious attachment might feel in a mental whirlpool. A simple late text message can set off a chain of insecurities that leave them in a state of fear and anxiety. We will learn more about anxious attachment and the anxiety that often tangles the hearts of people who have this style of attachment. More importantly, we will look at the ways to understand, heal, and build strong bonds.

• • • • • • • • • •

The Anxious Mindset

Anxious attachment in adults shows up as a certain way of thinking and acting that comes from having deep-seated fears and insecurities. Here is a more in-depth look at the anxious mindset and how it affects relationships:

1. **Trigger Sensitivity**: People who have anxious attachment are often very alert for signs that things might not be going well in their relationships. Actions, words, or even body language that could mean a threat to the stability of their relationship can easily set them off. Feelings of worry, panic, or fear can come from being too sensitive.[1]

2. **Self-Perception of Defectiveness**: Feeling like you're flawed or not deserving of love is one of the main beliefs that leads to anxious attachment. People who are anxiously attached often worry about being left alone and may keep looking for reassurance from their partners to calm their fears.[2]

3. **Overly Demanding or Clingy Behavior**: People who have anxious attachment may become too close to or needy with their partners in order to feel safe. They might need to talk to or affirm them often to feel safe in the relationship.[3]

4. **People-Pleasing Tendencies**: People who are anxiously attached often do things to please others because they want to keep the connection and avoid being rejected. Because of this, they might put up with bad behavior in relationships.[4]

5. **Lack of Trust**: Anxious attachment is characterized by problems with trust, which makes it hard for the person to relax into the relationship. This makes them act in ways that try to control their anxiety.[5]

6. **Reactivity to Criticism**: People who are anxiously attached often react strongly to criticism or perceived slights, which can make their fears and anxieties worse.[6]

These traits make it easier for anxiety and relationship problems to keep happening. The anxiously attached person needs closeness and reassurance to ease their insecurities, but their actions may push their partners away, which reinforces their fears of being left alone or not being good enough.

Recognizing these patterns is the first step to becoming more self-aware, which is very important for people who want to change their attachment style to one that feels safer. People who have anxious attachment can break the cycle of insecurity and build healthier, more fulfilling relationships by figuring out and dealing with the causes of their worries.

· · · ● ● · ● ● · ·

Skill-Building Techniques

Both the person who is dealing with anxious attachment and their partner may find it difficult to get through the rough waters of this attachment style. Anxious attachment is characterized by a strong fear of being left alone and an intense need for approval and comfort. This is often caused by not getting enough consistent care as a child, which can lead to feelings of insecurity that can grow into full-blown anxious attachment as an adult. People with this attachment style often think too much, are very good at spotting the smallest signs of disinterest or rejection, and can make the worst possible assumptions about harmless behaviors.

A lot of different self-awareness, self-regulation, and skill-building techniques are needed to deal with anxious attachment patterns and make relationships healthier. Let's look at a set of exercises that can help people deal with their anxious attachment tendencies and paint their relationships with colors of stability and calm.

1. **Mindfulness and Meditation:**
   The meditation practice of mindfulness is like learning how to be still when your mind is full of worrying thoughts. Meditation involves focusing on the present moment without judging it. Watching your thoughts and feelings come and go like waves in the shore of your mind is like recognizing them but not jumping in. By putting a pause between their feelings and reactions, practicing mindfulness can help people with anxious attachment have a more balanced response to emotional triggers.[7]

2. **Cognitive Reframing:**

With this method, you learn to see the glass as half full, even when your anxious thoughts try to tell you it's empty. Finding negative thought patterns and replacing them with more balanced or positive ones is what cognitive reframing is all about. It's possible to change the thought "They didn't text back, they must be losing interest" to "They might be busy; I know they care about me."

3. **Therapy:**

Going to therapy can be like having a guide show you the way through the maze of anxious attachment. It gives you a safe place to talk about attachment triggers, learn better ways to deal with stress, and work on building stronger attachments. Therapy gives people the chance to really understand where their anxious attachment patterns come from and work through them in a safe and structured setting.

4. **Communication Skills Training:**

Mastering the art of communication is one of the most important things you can do to deal with anxious attachment. To do this, you need to be able to clearly and non-reactively state your needs, fears, and wants, as well as learn to listen actively and create a safer and more open line of communication with your partner. You should learn how to ask for reassurance in a healthy way instead of letting fear control how you act.

5. **Self-Compassion Practices:**

Self-compassion means recognizing how you feel, being kind to yourself, and knowing that you're not the only one going through hard times. It means talking to yourself in a kinder way and letting yourself grow and change at your own pace.

6. **Regular Physical Exercise:**

Working out can be a very effective way to deal with stress. Being active on a regular basis can help you deal with anxiety symptoms, boost your mood, and make you healthier overall.

7. **Good Sleep Habits:**

Making sure you get enough restful sleep is very important because not getting enough sleep can make anxiety and emotional reactions worse. Setting up a regular sleep schedule and making your bedroom a good place to sleep can have a big effect on your ability to deal with anxious attachment tendencies.

8. **Relaxation Techniques:**
Deep breathing, progressive muscle relaxation, and guided imagery are some techniques that can help calm an anxious mind and ease the physical symptoms that come with it.

9. **Creating a Support Network:**
Having understanding friends and family can be a safety net of reassurance and validation that can help ease the fears and insecurities that come with anxious attachment.

All of these exercises and techniques are just a small part of a bigger plan to help people with anxious attachment disorders have better, more satisfying relationships. Also, don't forget that the goal isn't to be perfect, but to make progress every step, breath, and moment.

• • • • ● • ● • • •

Real-Life Examples

Sophia is a young professional who has always been worried about how her relationships are going. Her phone's unread text messages often felt like time bombs, and every minute of silence made her fear of being left alone stronger. Sophia knew that her anxiety was making it hard for her to make real connections with other people, so she chose to go to therapy. She learned about anxious attachment in her sessions and started doing exercises to help her mind and body calm down whenever she felt anxious. These small, steady steps helped Sophia deal with her fears less impulsively and tell her partner what she needed better.

Then there's Ethan, who had always judged his own worth by how other people saw him, especially when it came to relationships. He felt like he could see his whole emotional world in the self-help book on anxious attachment it was that good. Ethan started going to a local support group for people with anxious attachment disorder. There, he learned how to control himself and boost his self-esteem. By showing himself kindness and putting up healthy boundaries, Ethan gradually felt safe within himself, which made his relationships better.

Amanda and Patrick, a married couple, were caught in the rough waves of anxious and avoidant attachment dynamics. Their fights often left them feeling emotionally drained, with Amanda's stress and Patrick's withdrawal making things worse. They chose to go to couples therapy, where they learned about different types of attachment and how their fears made them act the way they did. They broke the cycle of anxiety and avoidance by doing exercises to improve their communication and learn about each other's triggers. This led to a more secure and understanding relationship.

In the last part of this chapter, it's important to stress the encouraging truth: anxious attachment is not a terminal diagnosis; it's a way to grow as a person and in relationships. Realizing that you have an anxious attachment style is the first thing that you can do to make your relationships safer and more satisfying.

The stories of Sophia, Ethan, Amanda, and Patrick show how self-awareness and practical strategies can change your life. They show that anyone can get through the rough waters of anxious attachment and reach the calmer shores of secure attachment if they have the right tools and a supportive environment.

There may be hard parts on the path, and at times it may feel like a test of your strength. With each step forward, however, the cloud of worry lifts a little, revealing more clear skies of understanding, compassion, and self-confidence.

$$\bullet \ \bullet \ \bullet \ \bullet \ \bullet \ \bullet \ \bullet \ \bullet \ \bullet$$

Workbook Section: Navigating Anxious Attachment

1. Reflection: Your Mind's Echo

Reflect on a recent instance where a small incident or misunderstanding spiraled into anxiety or fear regarding the stability of your relationship. Jot down the incident, your initial feelings, the thoughts that followed, and how it affected your behavior and interaction with your partner.

2. Mindfulness Breathing Exercise:

Practice a 5-minute mindfulness breathing exercise. Sit comfortably, close your eyes, and focus solely on your breath. As thoughts come, acknowledge them and let them float away, returning your focus to your breath.

- How did you feel before and after the exercise?

- Did practicing mindfulness help in alleviating any anxious thoughts, even momentarily?

3. Cognitive Reframing Challenge:

Identify a recurring negative thought pattern that often emerges in your relationships. Now, practice reframing this thought into a more balanced or positive perspective.

- Note down the negative thought, and beside it, write down the reframed thought.

- Reflect on how this new perspective could alter your emotional reaction in a similar future scenario.

4. Active Communication Exercise:

With a trusted individual, practice expressing a concern or fear without blame or assumption. Use "I" statements to express how certain actions or situations make you feel.

- Reflect on the experience:

  - How did it feel to communicate in this manner?

  - How did the individual respond?

5. Self-Compassion Journaling:

Journal about a recent situation where anxious attachment manifested. Extend compassion towards yourself as you write, understanding that these reactions come from a place of fear and past experiences.

- Write a comforting or understanding statement to yourself to conclude your journaling.

6. Boundary-Setting Exercise:

Reflect on your relationships and identify areas where you might be overextending yourself to please others or to keep the peace.

- List down some healthy boundaries you could set to protect your emotional well-being.

7. Support Circle:

Identify a small circle of supportive and understanding individuals in your life.

- Write down their names and the qualities or actions that make them a supportive presence in your life.

8. Therapy Exploration:

If you're open to it, explore the option of therapy to work through anxious attachment tendencies.

- Research local therapists or online counseling services specializing in attachment issues.

9. Celebrate Progress:

Reflect on any progress, no matter how small, you've made in understanding or navigating your anxious attachment.

- Write down at least one instance of progress and celebrate this step towards healthier attachment.

10. Empathy and Understanding:

Reflect on the stories of Sophia, Ethan, Amanda, and Patrick.

- Which story resonated with you the most and why?

- What aspects of their journey could you incorporate into your own path towards secure attachment?

12. Group Discussion or Individual Reflection:

Engage in a group discussion or individual reflection on the journey from anxious to secure attachment as outlined in the chapter.

- Share personal experiences, challenges, and victories on this journey.

---

1. https://ncrw.org/anxious-attachment-triggers/

2. https://www.simplypsychology.org/how-to-move-from-anxious-attachment-to-secure.html

3. https://www.psychologytoday.com/us/blog/addiction-and-recovery/202009/recognizing-the-anxious-attachment-style

4. https://psychcentral.com/health/anxious-attachment-style-signs

5. https://therapist.com/relationships/how-to-overcome-anxious-attachment-style/

6. https://www.psychologytoday.com/us/blog/addiction-and-recovery/202009/recognizing-the-anxious-attachment-style

7. https://www.attachmentproject.com/blog/self-regulation-anxious-attachment-triggers/

CHAPTER TWELVE

THE COMPLEXITIES OF AVOIDANT ATTACHMENT AS AN ADULT

Adrian is the embodiment of self-sufficiency. He is proud of being able to deal with life's problems on his own. He loves being alone more than anything else, and his motto is *"I've got this."* Adrian basically never shows how he feels; he usually keeps them to himself.

Adrian's partners often call him a "lone wolf" when they're together. He is very good at keeping his cool, even when things are getting heated. Adrian's lack of emotional connection often makes it seem like he doesn't care about his partners, who want a deeper emotional connection that Adrian either can't or won't give them.

When things get tough in a relationship, he tends to pull away. He likes having his own space and taking care of things by himself. People who want to get closer to him sometimes feel turned off by his desire to avoid getting emotionally involved.

His story shows how someone with an avoidant attachment style lives. For this person, emotional distance is a safe place to be, and the thought of being close to someone is like a threat to his independence. Adrian's story sets the scene for our journey through the confusing world of avoidant attachment, looking into its many facets, learning where it comes from, and discovering ways to find safer and more satisfying connections.

• • • ● ●• • ● ● •• •

The Avoidant's Emotional Armor

When someone is avoidant attached, they often use a variety of defense mechanisms to deal with the emotional ups and downs of relationships. These defenses are meant to keep them from being vulnerable and to give them some control over their emotional world. People who suffer from avoidant attachment often have a strong desire for independence and self-sufficiency. This may be a way for them to protect themselves from the perceived dangers of intimacy.

One way to do this is to master the art of suppression, which means pushing emotions, especially ones that hint at any kind of dependence, to the edges of your mind. They learn not only how to hide their need for closeness but also how to dull the pain that comes with showing emotions. But suppression is not the only weapon in the fight against weakness. There is often denial that goes along with it, an unwillingness to accept the basic human needs and wants.[1]

A lot of different ways to stay away from someone are used in the fight against intimacy. Attachment theory came up with the term "deactivating strategies" to describe what they might do. One example is taking attention away from attachment needs when they are being met. This could show up as focusing on their partner's flaws when they feel close to them or by getting lost in hobbies and tasks that take their mind off of their feelings.

Moreover, the lack of closeness can extend to memories; people who suffer from avoidant attachment may selectively remember experiences connected to attachment. They may not remember as much about personal or emotional events or experiences that would normally make them feel attached or longing.

The story of avoidant attachment shows how flexible and protective people can be, even if it means giving up closeness and deep connections. Still, it's important to remember that, no matter what attachment style someone is using, deep down they still want to connect and be close to someone. It is brave to go from the safe harbor of detachment to the rough but rewarding waters of emotional intimacy. Peeling back the layers of defense and fostering secure attachment is a journey from the known to the unknown.

• • • • ●•● • • • •

Exercises for Opening Up

People who avoid situations often put on a suit of emotional armor that was expertly made to protect them from the threat of being vulnerable. Under this tough exterior lies a desire for connection, though it's overshadowed by the fear of being rejected or suffocated. When you want sweets but are worried about cavities, it's like that. How then does one walk this tricky line between keeping your guard up and letting yourself be emotionally available? Here's a map to help you get around this area:

1. **Self-Reflection**: Being aware is the first step toward change. People who tend to avoid things might benefit from reflecting on themselves to learn more about their fears and defenses. It can be enlightening to think about past relationships and see patterns.

2. **Therapy**: Going to therapy can be very helpful for people who avoid things. It lets you look at your deepest fears and work through them in a safe place.

3. **Mindfulness and Relaxation Techniques**: These techniques can help you deal with anxiety and become more aware of your feelings. Mindfulness meditation, yoga, and exercises that help you relax can be very helpful.

4. **Expressive Writing**: Writing about how you feel and what you've been through can be helpful. It helps people deal with their feelings and understand why they act the way they do.

5. **Learning to Communicate Needs**: Learning to express one's needs and wants in relationships is crucial for avoidant people. A key step can be to practice being assertive in your communication.

6. **Taking Small Risks**: Avoidant people could begin by being vulnerable and

taking small risks. It could be as easy as expressing a need or a fear.

7. **Exploring New Relationships**: Forging new relationships can sometimes give you a clean slate to try new things and break old habits.

8. **Physical Touch**: A simple hug or a pat on the back can sometimes help people get over their problems. Being more emotionally available can be aided by doing things that encourage touch and closeness.

9. **Mindful Listening and Responding**: It is crucial to practice listening with awareness and responding rather than reacting. It enables a deeper understanding and connection with others.

10. **Joining Support Groups**: Engaging with others who share similar attachment concerns can provide a supportive community to work through challenges.

11. **Practicing Patience and Compassion**: Change takes time and work. During this process, it is essential to exercise patience and kindness toward oneself and others.

12. **Exploring Emotional Triggers**: Finding out what makes you withdraw emotionally and working through those triggers can be a life-changing exercise.

13. **Accepting and Expressing Emotions**: Learning to accept and express emotions in a healthy way is a significant step towards becoming more emotionally available.

14. **Book Reading and Workshops**: Reading books about attachment and relationships, going to workshops, and learning new things all the time can give you new insights and tools for change.

These exercises are not a one-size-fits-all solution, but rather a tailor's rack full of options. Some exercises may resonate and be more powerful for some people than others. The journey to becoming more emotionally available is one of personal discovery, challenges, and, ultimately, growth. Through these exercises, avoidant people can slowly but surely chip away at their emotional armor, revealing the soft, connective tissue of real relationships that lie beneath.

It's important to remember that avoidant attachment patterns are not indelible marks on the mind. With perseverance, self-compassion, and the right help, they can be changed. If we're brave enough to go into the sometimes scary territory of our inner world, our emotional landscapes can change.

The journey may be difficult and the path may have its share of thorns, but the reward—a life with better relationships and a more secure attachment style—is well worth the effort.

Workbook Section: Unraveling the Avoidant Armor

1. Reflection: The Lone Wolf Syndrome

- Reflect on moments in your relationships where you've pulled away emotionally or physically when things got tough.

- Describe the situation, your reactions, and the impact it had on your relationship.

- Were there instances where your 'lone wolf' tendencies came to the forefront?

2. Expressive Writing: The Armor's Origin

- Engage in a 20-minute writing exercise where you explore the origins of your emotional armor.

- Reflect on your childhood, past relationships, or any significant events that might have contributed to your avoidant attachment tendencies.

- What specific memories come to mind when you think about times you've emotionally distanced yourself from someone close to you?

- Can you recall a moment from your childhood where you felt the urge to guard your feelings? Why do you think that moment stands out?

- How would you describe the metaphorical walls you've constructed over the years? Why were they built, and how have they changed with time?

- When was the last time you genuinely felt connected to someone without any barriers? What made that moment different?

- Try to remember a situation when someone tried to get closer to you emotionally and you pulled away. How do you think they felt during that moment?

- Are there past relationships or friendships that might have been affected or even ended because of your avoidant behaviors? What would you say to those individuals now, given the chance?

- If you could rewrite your story of attachment, what would the ideal version look like? How would your interactions and relationships be different?

- When discussing emotional topics or facing confrontations, how does your body react? Are there specific sensations you've noticed that signal a retreat or avoidance?

- What are the fears or beliefs that hold you back from fully connecting with others? Have they changed over time?

- When you think about the concept of vulnerability, what images or scenarios come to mind? Why do you think those specific images emerge?

3. Mindfulness Meditation: Tuning Into Emotions

- Practice a 10-minute mindfulness meditation focusing on your breath.

- As you breathe, tune into any emotions that arise. Instead of pushing them away, just observe them without judgment.

- Reflect on what emotions were easy or difficult to sit with.

4. Communication Challenge: Expressing Needs

- Identify a need or desire you have within a close relationship that you've kept to yourself.

- Practice expressing this need to the person involved in a clear and assertive manner.

- Reflect on the experience: How did it feel to express your needs? How was your expression received?

5. Therapy Exploration:

- If open to it, consider seeking a therapist specializing in attachment issues.

- Reflect on any fears or reservations you have about therapy.

- If already in therapy, reflect on any insights or progress you've made concerning your avoidant attachment tendencies.

6. Small Risks: Practice Vulnerability

- Identify small ways in which you can practice vulnerability in your relationships.

- It could be sharing a fear, expressing a need, or showing affection.

- Reflect on each experience: How did it feel to be vulnerable?

- What reactions did you observe from others?

7. Exploring Triggers:

- List down scenarios or behaviors that trigger your tendency to withdraw or put up your emotional armor.

- Reflect on why these particular triggers affect you and how you might respond differently in the future.

8. Mindful Listening Exercise:

- Engage in a conversation with a close one where you practice mindful listening.

- Instead of planning your responses, just listen with full attention.

- Reflect on the experience: Did you discover anything new?

- How did it impact the conversation?

9. Physical Touch: Experiment with Connection

- With a trusted individual, practice engaging in more physical touch, like hugs or holding hands.

- Reflect on how physical touch affects your emotional connection.

10. Reflection on Progress:

- Reflect on any progress you've made in understanding or navigating your avoidant attachment.

- Celebrate small victories, no matter how minor they may seem.

11. Navigating New Relationships:

- If applicable, reflect on how understanding your attachment style has impacted your approach to new relationships.

- Note any changes in your behavior or emotional responses.

12. Self-Compassion Meditation:

- Practice a self-compassion meditation.

- Reflect on how cultivating self-compassion can support your journey towards more secure attachment.

---

1. https://mauimindfultherapy.com/neuroscience-attachment-theory

CHAPTER THIRTEEN

THE ENIGMA OF DISORGANIZED/FEARFUL-AVOIDANT ATTACHMENT AS AN ADULT

Disorganized attachment can feel like being lost in a maze with shifting walls. Consider Belinda, who frequently gets stuck in a cycle where she wants to be close to her partner but feels suffocated when he does. Her emotions are unpredictable, which makes her and her partner both angry and confused. Belinda's story is a live demonstration of how disorganized attachment can turn the emotional landscape into a maze of conflicting needs and fears, making it a difficult puzzle for both the person going through it and the people who are trying to understand it.

• • • • • • • • • •

Characteristics and Conflicts

A combination of ambivalence and confusion characterizes the disorganized or fearful - avoidant attachment style. A push-and-pull dynamic in relationships is frequently reflected in the behaviors of people with this attachment style. Here is a look at the complicated world of disorganized attachment:

1. **Ambivalence**: A sense of ambivalence is at the heart of disorganized attachment. People are frequently torn between wanting to be close to someone and wanting to be far away from them. This conflicted desire is similar to how they felt when they wanted safety but were afraid of the people who could give it to them, usually their caregivers when they were young.

2. **Fear of Intimacy**: There is a strong fear of intimacy, which is often a defense mechanism to protect oneself from the rejection or abandonment they fear. They want to be emotionally close to people, but the thought of being vulnerable can be scary, so they might push people away to protect themselves.

3. **Confusing Signals**: Both themselves and others may be perplexed by the signals they send. When closeness is achieved, they may push away despite showing a need for it. Not only for them, but also for their partners, this push-pull dynamic can be confusing.

4. **Erratic Behavior**: Their behavior can be unpredictable and erratic. They may crave closeness one moment and distance the next. This can make them and the people around them feel a whirlwind of emotions.

5. **Unresolved Trauma**: At its core, the disorganized attachment style is often caused by unresolved trauma from previous relationships or bad experiences in childhood. This unresolved trauma can show up as a fear of making connections or a failure to maintain relationships.

6. **Low Self-Esteem**: Low self-esteem frequently goes hand in hand with disorganized attachment, and it can be caused by early experiences of rejection or inconsistent caregiving. This low self-esteem may make fears of rejection or abandonment even worse.

7. **Overwhelming Emotions**: The emotional landscape can be quite rocky, and strong feelings often come to the surface. These feelings can be hard to control, which can cause more stress.

8. **Avoidance and Anxiety**: They frequently show signs of both avoidant attachment style and anxious attachment style, which results in an amalgam of conflicting behaviors and emotions.

9. **Hyper-vigilance**: Even in relationships that seem safe, they might be extremely alert and always looking for signs of rejection or abandonment.

For those who have disorganized attachment and the people who are close to them, these traits paint a picture of an intricate, frequently stressful emotional environment. Conflicting actions and feelings are often a result of traumas and fears from the past, which causes people to act in a self-protective but isolating way in relationships. A better understanding of these traits can help people and their therapists work through these problems and work toward a more secure attachment style.

$$\cdot \ \bullet \ \bullet \ \bullet \ \bullet \ \bullet \ \bullet \ \bullet \ \bullet \ \cdot$$

The Root Causes

The root causes of disorganized or fearful - avoidant attachment are frequently rocky childhood experiences where the soil of emotional security was never fertile. This attachment style frequently takes root during the inconsistent and occasionally chaotic early emotional interactions.

Imagine a young tree trying to establish its roots in a patch of land that goes from being parched dry to being flooded. This is similar to the emotional world of a child who develops a disorganized attachment style. The caregivers are inconsistent; sometimes they are present and helpful, and other times they are absent or even harmful. In a psychological sense, this erratic caregiving is like the weather that the young tree has to deal with, making it difficult to form a strong, stable attachment.

Children who have gone through this often find themselves in a tough spot. In terms of attachment, their natural instinct is to look for comfort and safety in the people who care for them. But the thing that makes us feel safe is also what makes us feel afraid and upset.

A complex, fearful - avoidant attachment style that can last into adult relationships is set up by this contradictory pull-and-push dynamic.

Caretakers' inconsistent responsiveness or, in some cases, harmful interactions can hinder the development of a safe foundation from which the child can explore the world. Instead of being a playground, the world turns into a battlefield where emotional landmines could go off at any time.

The effects of this early attachment experience last into adulthood and influence how people with disorganized attachment handle relationships. Fear and mistrust, along with competing needs for closeness and safety, make for a complicated and often turbulent emotional landscape that needs careful attention and help to get through.

Disorganized attachment can develop for a number of reasons, not the least of which is inconsistent caregiving. Trauma, in all of its forms, can also play a big part. Childhood traumas like abuse, neglect, or loss can leave emotional scars that make it hard to form secure, stable attachments.

Understanding the underlying causes of disorganized attachment involves looking at how early emotional experiences, caregiver relationships, and maybe even trauma interact. Not only for those who experience disorganized attachment, but also for their loved ones and therapists who want to help them on a path toward more secure, stable emotional connections, untangling this web is essential.

• • • ● ● ● ● ● • •

Strategies for Stability

It's not easy to get through the maze of fearful or disorganized - avoidant attachment. It's a journey that calls for a map, a compass, and a lot of fortitude. Finding some sort of stability can feel like trying to find a radio signal in a storm for people with this attachment style who are constantly experiencing conflicting emotions. But with the right tactics, you can turn down the noise and find a clearer channel of emotional connection.

   1. **Mindfulness and Meditation:**

- Mindfulness meditation encourages a non-judgmental awareness of the present moment, which can be especially helpful in managing the emotional volatility associated with disorganized attachment.

- Practicing mindfulness can help individuals become more aware of their emotional triggers and responses, making it easier to manage them in a healthy way.

2. **Therapy:**

- Therapy, particularly trauma-informed therapy or therapies focused on attachment, can be incredibly beneficial.

- A therapist can help unravel the complex threads of past experiences and present behaviors, aiding in the development of healthier coping strategies.

3. **Journaling:**

- Journaling can provide a means of self-reflection, helping individuals explore their emotions, reactions, and behaviors in a safe, private space.

- It's a self-paced way to explore one's emotional landscape and can provide insights that might be discussed further in therapy.

4. **Support Groups:**

- Finding a community of individuals who share similar attachment concerns can provide a sense of belonging and understanding.

- Support groups, whether in person or online, can offer a platform for sharing experiences and coping strategies.

5. **Creating Consistency:**

- Establishing a consistent routine, including a consistent response to emotional triggers, can provide a sense of stability.

- Consistency can help in creating a predictable environment which is often lacking in the lives of individuals with disorganized attachment.

6. **Self-compassion:**

- Developing self-compassion is crucial. It's important to recognize that the journey towards emotional stability is a process, not an event.

- Celebrating small victories and being gentle with oneself during setbacks can foster a sense of progress and motivation.

7. **Relaxation Techniques:**

- Techniques such as deep breathing, yoga, or progressive muscle relaxation can be helpful in managing anxiety and emotional volatility.

- These techniques can provide a go-to toolkit for managing stressful situations or emotional upheavals.

For those with disorganized attachment, the path to emotional stability may have more turns and twists than a mountain pass, but with the right tools, it's doable. It is possible to promote a greater sense of emotional stability and healthier attachment dynamics through a combination of self-awareness, therapeutic support, education, and practical coping strategies.

A complex challenge is presented by disorganized attachment, which has a maze of emotions and behaviors that don't match. It's a dance between wanting to be close to someone and being afraid of it. It can be difficult to untangle the inner turmoil that is frequently reflected in the chaos of relationships. Despite this complexity, there is room for understanding and development. Even though the above strategies can help, the journey may often need the help of a professional therapist who can guide you through the confusing web of emotions and behaviors. Individuals can move toward a place of greater emotional stability and healthier interpersonal connections by working through the underlying causes of their disorganized attachment with the help of a skilled professional and therapeutic exploration. A more secure attachment landscape is possible with the right help and resources, despite the winding path.

• • • • ● • ● • • •

Workbook Section: Navigating the Labyrinth of Disorganized Attachment

1. Reflection: The Push-and-Pull

- Reflect on moments where you've experienced the push-and-pull dynamic in your relationships.

- Describe the situation, your emotions, and the reactions of those involved.

- How did this dynamic affect the relationship?

2. Meditation Practice: Centering Amidst the Storm

- Engage in a daily 10-minute mindfulness meditation to observe your thoughts and emotions without judgment.

- Take note of any recurring fears or conflicting desires that arise.

3. Expressive Writing: The Echoes of the Past

- Engage in a 20-minute writing exercise exploring any childhood experiences or past traumas that might be influencing your current attachment style.

- Reflect on any patterns you notice.

4. Role-Play: Practicing New Responses

- With a trusted individual or in a therapeutic setting, engage in role-play to practice new responses in relationship scenarios that trigger your disorganized attachment tendencies.

5. Visioning: Imagining Secure Attachment

- Engage in a visualization exercise where you imagine yourself in secure attachment scenarios.

- What does it feel like?

- Write down your experiences and discuss them in therapy or a trusted support setting.

CHAPTER FOURTEEN

EXERCISES FOR ALL ATTACHMENT STYLES THAT AREN'T DULL AS DISHWATER

The path to self-improvement frequently includes a number of questionnaires, but let's be honest: a dull set of questions can make the process feel like waiting for paint to dry. This task, however, can turn into an interesting journey of self-discovery if approached with a bit of creativity and enthusiasm. Who says exploring the depths of your mind has to be as dull as a snail race? With the right exercises, it can be as exciting as a plot twist in a thriller book. So, let's start this journey with some unusual exercises that promise to keep you on your toes and move you closer to a secure attachment style. The path to self-discovery doesn't have to be boring; it can be as exciting and fun as a carnival!

Skill-Building Activities

Let's leave the ordinary behind and enter a world where exploring oneself is both fascinating and educational. Here are a bunch of exercises to help you figure out your attachment style and make the process as stimulating as a strong coffee on a lazy morning.

1. **Role-Reversal Exercise:**

   - Participate in this educational activity with a dependable friend or partner.

Play each other in situations that brought up attachment worries or fears from previous relationships. The goal is to learn how you might come across to others and how they might come across to you. It's like walking a mile in someone else's emotional shoes.

○ This exercise is comparable to stepping into a living, breathing model of another person's emotional world. You can learn more about your own patterns and how they might affect your relationships by acting out each other's actions and reactions in particular situations. Performance is not important; perception and comprehension are. Insights into how your attachment style shows up in interactions can be gained from your partner's feedback.

2. **Attachment Storyboarding**:

○ Make a storyboard for your attachment. To represent important people, events, and feelings throughout your life, use drawings, photographs, or even magazine cutouts. It's a visual tour of your attachment history that can help you understand and talk about your patterns.

○ Visual storytelling is a powerful way to travel the back roads of your emotional history. By making a storyboard, you essentially create a visual narrative of your attachment journey, noticing patterns, important events, and influential people along the way. It's like talking to your past, visualizing how your attachment style started and changed over time.

3. **Emotional Vocabulary Expansion**:

○ Lack of words to express our feelings frequently prevents us from expressing ourselves. Try to use a new word that describes an emotion in a sentence every day. It's about expanding your emotional vocabulary, which can lead to deeper connections.

4. **Expressive Arts**:

○ Expressive arts, like painting, dancing, writing, or making music, can help you understand and express your feelings better. Make a piece of art that shows your emotional state or your relationships. It's calming and educational!

○ Engaging in expressive arts is like giving your inner world the mic and letting it tell its stories through color, movement, or melody. It's a nonverbal conversation between you and your emotions that helps you better understand your attachment style. Making something new can be freeing, giving you a sense of relief and a way to learn about yourself.

5. **Interactive Journaling**:

○ This is not your average diary entry. Engage in a dialog with yourself on paper. Ask questions about your fears, desires, and your relationships, and answer them as honestly as possible. Alternatively, have a trusted person respond to your entries to gain different perspectives.

○ This activity turns journaling into a conversation. You can learn more about yourself by asking yourself questions about your fears, wants, and patterns in relationships and then responding to those questions. Having someone you trust respond to your entries can also give you fresh ideas that can help you understand things better.

6. **Themed Discussion Nights**:

○ Host a themed discussion night with close friends or a support group where you discuss attachment, relationships, and personal growth. It's a feast for the mind, with lots of friendship and shared knowledge.

○ A communal space for shared learning and reflection is created by facilitating discussions on topics related to attachment and relationships. On this path to self-discovery, sharing your experiences and ideas can help you understand things better and give you a sense of community.

7. **Book Club with a Twist**:

○ Create a book club that reads books about psychology and self-help. Sharing different points of view on attachment with other people can help you learn new things and grow as a person.

8. **Couples' Attachment Workshops**:

   - Attending a workshop for couples can be a fun and educational way to work on building a secure attachment with your partner.

9. **Adventure Therapy**:

   - Take part in outdoor activities or challenges that push you outside of your comfort zone and promote trust, communication, and emotional expression.

   - A unique combination of adrenaline, trust-building, and self-reflection is adventure therapy. By doing things or facing challenges outside, you not only get out of your comfort zone but also build trust, communication, and emotional expression, all of which are important for understanding and improving your attachment style.

10. **Virtual Reality Scenarios**:

    - Utilize cutting-edge technology, such as virtual reality, to create relationship simulations that offer a secure environment for experimenting with new emotional and communication techniques.

11. **Therapeutic Board Games**:

    - You won't believe it, but there are board games that are made to help you learn more about yourself and how to get along with others. Games like "The Ungame" and "Therapy the Game" can be both entertaining and educational.

These exercises are designed to bring to light the parts of your attachment style that are often hidden, while also making sure that the process is as interesting as a great movie. So jump in and let the waves of self-discovery carry you to shores of deeper understanding and improved attachment.

• • • ● ● • ● • • •

Relationship Scenarios

Finding our way through the maze of relationships often involves situations that make us react in ways that show our attachment preferences. These made-up situations are meant to help you see and understand your natural reactions. There are reflection questions after each scenario to help you think more deeply about your responses and what they might say about your attachment style.

1. **Scenario: Unexpected Silence**:

   - Imagine that one morning your partner, with whom you have a daily ritual of texting "good morning," stops responding. It's already afternoon and there's no message from them.

     - Reflective Questions:

       - What are your initial thoughts?

       - How does this scenario make you feel?

       - How would you likely respond?

2. **Scenario: A Friend's Cancellation**:

   - You've been looking forward to dinner with a close friend all week, but they have to cancel at the last minute due to an emergency at work.

     - Reflective Questions:

       - What's your immediate emotional reaction?

       - How do you manage your disappointment?

       - What would be your response to your friend?

3. Scenario: Critical Feedback:

- Your partner gives you some honest but kind feedback about a behavior of yours that has been bothering them.

  - Reflective Questions:

    - How do you receive this feedback?

    - What emotions does this scenario evoke?

    - How might your attachment style influence your response?

4. Scenario: Parental Expectations:

- Your parent expresses disappointment that you've chosen a career path they don't approve of.

  - Reflective Questions:

    - How do you feel about their disappointment?

    - How does this scenario affect your self-esteem or self-worth?

    - How would you communicate with your parent about this?

5. Scenario: New Relationship Energy:

- You've started dating someone new and feel excited but also vulnerable about the growing intimacy.

  - Reflective Questions:

    - How do you navigate your vulnerability?

    - What fears, if any, does this new relationship stir?

    - How do you communicate your needs and boundaries?

6. Scenario: Reconnecting with an Ex:

- An ex-partner reaches out wanting to catch up over coffee, and you feel a mix of curiosity and apprehension.

- Reflective Questions:

    ○ How do you feel about this outreach?

    ○ What boundaries would you set for this meet-up?

    ○ How does your attachment style play into your willingness or hesitance?

7. **Scenario: Work-life Balance Challenge**:

    ○ Your partner has been working late every night for a week, and you feel neglected.

    - Reflective Questions:

        ○ How do you cope with the feeling of neglect?

        ○ How do you communicate your needs to your partner?

        ○ How does this scenario reflect on your attachment fears or insecurities?

Each situation is a vignette, a small piece of your relationship life that shows how your attachment dynamics work. The purpose of the reflective questions is to help you become more self-aware and to better understand how your attachment style shows up in different types of relationships.

Journal Prompts

When done with an open mind and curiosity, journaling can be like talking to your inner self. It's about exploring the depths of your emotional landscape and coming up with insights that could both teach you something new and change your life. The following questions are meant to help you on this journey inside, to push and prod you, and to encourage a deep reflection that goes beyond the surface.

1. **Exploring Your Emotional Echoes**:

   ○ Describe a moment where you felt a strong emotional reaction in a relationship. What were the triggers? What past experiences does it remind you of?

2. **The Nature of Your Bonds**:

   ○ Reflect on the relationships that have had the most impact on your life. How have these relationships shaped your expectations and behaviors in your current relationships?

3. **Unpacking Your Suitcase**:

   ○ If your emotional baggage could talk, what tales would it tell? What have you packed away that continues to weigh on your present?

4. **The Mirror of Relationships**:

   ○ What aspects of yourself have you discovered through your interactions with others? How have your relationships mirrored your fears, desires, or unresolved conflicts?

5. **Your Relationship Blueprint**:

   ○ Reflect on the patterns that seem to recur in your relationships. What are the common themes, and how do they correlate with your attachment style?

6. **Navigating Your Emotional Storms**:

   ○ Describe a time when your emotions felt like a tempest in a teacup. What calmed the storm, and what fueled it?

7. **The Faces of Your Attachment**:

   ○ How does your attachment style manifest in different relationships – with family, friends, and romantic partners? Are there variations, and if so, what influences them?

8. **Your Attachment Evolution**:

  ○ Reflect on how your attachment style has evolved over time. What events or insights catalyzed these changes?

9. **The Dance of Intimacy**:

  ○ Explore your comfort levels with intimacy and vulnerability. What steps lead you closer to or farther from an emotionally connected dance with others?

10. **Your Ideal Relational Space**:

  ○ Describe the relational environment where you feel most secure and authentic. What elements contribute to creating this space, and how can you cultivate them in your present relationships?

11. **Your Self-Soothing Strategies**:

  ○ How do you manage distress or discomfort in relationships? Reflect on the effectiveness and adaptiveness of your self-soothing strategies.

12. **The Narrative of Your Needs**:

  ○ Explore your ability to express and meet your needs in relationships. How does your attachment style influence this narrative?

Each of these prompts is an invitation to explore your inner landscape and learn more about the experiences, feelings, and relationships that make up your attachment story. Remember as you write your reflections that this is not about having the right or wrong answers, but rather about starting a journey of self-discovery, one prompt at a time.

The journey to secure attachment is more of a spiral ascent than a sprint to the finish line. It involves going back, reevaluating, and improving. The exercises in this chapter are meant to be used as tools that you can use over and over again, with each visit possibly revealing new layers of insight as you grow. As you get older, your relationships change, and you learn more about your attachment style, doing these exercises again can give you new insights and improve your relationship skills. They are your constant companions on this journey, giving you a place to think about your inner relationships and develop a more secure attachment style over time. So, bookmark this chapter and give yourself the time and space to grow, while also being curious and patient. Remember that the path to secure attachment is not about racing to the finish line, but about having a conversation with yourself and others that lasts a lifetime.

CHAPTER FIFTEEN

How to Work on Your Attachment Style in Relationships

The amazing journey of exploring attachment styles within the context of romantic relationships. It's like deciding to finally clean out that closet that is way too cluttered. You know the one. It's been calling for a clean-up for a while, but just thinking about what's inside gives you chills. Still, one day, with a dash of resolve and a sprinkle of courage, you decide it's time. When you first open the closet doors, the sight is scary—more there's in there than you thought, and the tangled mess of forgotten scarves is a metaphor waiting to happen.

But as you get started and roll up your sleeves, something magical happens. You find things you forgot about and memories that make you smile among the dusty corners and piled-up memories. Yes, you find space, clarity, and a sense of order slowly emerging among the tangles. It's challenging, emotional, enlightening, and, dare I say it, liberating.

This is very similar to starting an investigation into and working on attachment styles in a relationship. It's about letting those feelings, fears, and desires out of their cluttered closet, facing the mess, and then slowly and tenderly starting to sort through it together. The process reveals patterns, triggers, and tender spots that need a gentle touch that you weren't aware of.

It's not a rom-com scene where rainbows herald the start of a new relationship. It's real, it's raw, and it takes a lot of patience, communication, and yes, a willingness to work through the mess together. But despite how scary it may be, the rewards are great. The journey is not only worthwhile but also deeply enriching because of the clarity, closeness, understanding, and strong foundation that result from this endeavor.

Communicating Your Needs

When attachment styles are taken into account, communication in relationships, especially when it comes to expressing needs and fears, can feel like navigating a minefield at times. However, it's important because good communication is the key to a happy, healthy relationship. It's the thing that brings two people together and helps them cross the sometimes huge gap between their different personal experiences, expectations, and feelings.

Understanding your attachment style is a crucial first step in this process because it provides a lens through which you can better understand not only how you interact with others but also how you express your needs and fears.

Because they were frequently met with understanding and support in their early life experiences, those with a secure attachment style may find it easier to express their needs and fears. However, the territory of expressing needs and fears can be more fraught with anxiety, fear of rejection, or discomfort for people with anxious, avoidant, or disorganized attachment styles.

A lot of research shows how important it is to use assertive communication, which means saying what you think, feel, and need in an open, honest, and respectful way. It's a skill that can be developed with practice and maybe a little courage.

Additionally, the fields of psychology and couple therapy give us tools like the "I" statements, which encourage a non-accusatory way of expressing one's feelings and needs. Instead of saying, "You never listen to me," which could make the other person defensive, say, "I feel unheard when we talk about important issues," which keeps the focus on your own experience and encourages understanding rather than defensiveness.

Along with "I" statements, practicing active listening is essential. This means not only listening to your partner, but also understanding and caring about their point of view. It's about creating a safe space where you can both feel seen, heard, and valued.

Mindfulness-based practices can also be helpful. Mindfulness can help you become more self-aware, which can make it easier to recognize and express your needs and fears. It can also help you understand and be patient with your partner's needs and fears.

And keep in mind that it's a journey. Similar to learning a new language, improving communication skills, especially when dealing with different attachment styles, takes time, practice, and a willingness to learn and grow together.

When it comes to relationships, navigating the areas of needs, fears, and effective communication while using the compass of knowing one's attachment style can lead to both personal growth and a deeper connection and understanding between partners.

· · · ● · ● ● · ·

Exercises for Couples

Reflecting on Differences and Similarities

Objective: Understanding and appreciating the unique and shared characteristics within the relationship.

1. **Materials Needed**: A sheet of paper and a pen for each person.

2. **Instructions**:

   ○ Separately, list down five traits or behaviors that you believe you bring to the relationship and five traits or behaviors your partner brings to the relationship.

   ○ Come together and share your lists. Discuss the similarities and differences, and how they contribute to your relationship.

- Reflect on how these traits interact with each other, especially when the waves get choppy.

Attachment Story Sharing

Objective: Gaining insight into each other's attachment history to foster understanding and empathy.

1. **Materials Needed**: A quiet, comfortable space, and an open heart.

2. **Instructions**:

- Take turns sharing your attachment stories. This includes experiences from childhood, past relationships, and pivotal moments that shaped your attachment style.

- Listen with an open heart and mind, resisting the urge to interject or offer solutions. The goal here is to understand and be understood.

Creating a Safe Haven

Objective: Establishing a secure and comforting environment for both individuals.

1. **Materials Needed**: A willingness to discuss and negotiate.

2. **Instructions**:

- Discuss what actions, behaviors, and environments make each of you feel safe and secure.

- Work together to create a "Safe Haven Agreement" that outlines how you'll ensure each other's emotional safety.

Exploring Triggers and Soothing Techniques

Objective: Identifying what triggers attachment fears and how to soothe each other.

1. **Materials Needed**: Pen and paper.

2. **Instructions**:

   - Independently jot down situations that trigger your attachment fears.

   - Share your lists and discuss.

   - Now, brainstorm and list soothing techniques that could help during these triggering situations.

The Attachment Playbook

Objective: Creating a go-to guide for navigating the attachment terrain in your relationship.

1. **Materials Needed**: A notebook or digital document.

2. **Instructions**:

   - Based on your discussions and insights from the previous exercises, create a playbook.

   - Include the identified triggers, soothing techniques, and your Safe Haven Agreement.

○ This playbook is a living document. Revisit and revise it as your relationship evolves and as you grow individually and together.

· · · ● ● · ● ● · · ·

The Listening Exercise:

Objective: Enhance listening skills and foster empathy.

1. **Materials Needed**: Just yourselves.

2. **Instructions**:

   ○ Decide who will speak first. The speaker will share something on their mind while the listener, well, listens.

   ○ The listener's job is to refrain from interrupting, offering solutions, or critiquing. Just listen.

   ○ Once the speaker has finished, the listener will reflect back on what they heard without adding their own interpretations.

   ○ Switch roles and repeat. This exercise helps in truly hearing and understanding each other.

Here's an example of how a conversation could be like:

- **Anna:** *(taking a deep breath)* "Alright, I'll go first. Lately, I've been feeling overwhelmed with work and balancing time with family. It seems like deadlines keep piling up and I barely get to spend quality time with Jake and Emma. I feel guilty about it, and sometimes I worry they'll resent me for always being 'too busy' for them."

- **Brian:** *(nodding attentively)* "So, from what you've shared, you've been feeling a lot of pressure due to the increasing workload. This has been taking a toll on the time you wish you could spend with Jake and Emma. You're concerned about them feeling neglected, and it's causing you guilt and anxiety."

- **Anna:** "Yes, that's exactly it. Thank you for listening."

- **Brian:** "Of course. Now, it's my turn. Remember, just listen."

- **Anna:** "I'm ready."

- **Brian:** "I've been trying to figure out a way to help around more. I've noticed you're stressed, and I want to be supportive. But I feel lost, unsure of how to assist without overstepping or making things more chaotic."

- **Anna:** "So you've observed the stress I've been under and you genuinely want to help out more. But you're a bit hesitant because you're not certain about the best ways to be supportive without inadvertently causing more confusion or stress."

- **Brian:** "Exactly. Thanks for understanding."

Through this exercise, Anna and Brian have offered each other a safe space to voice their feelings, ensuring they are on the same page and deepening their bond.

· · · ● · ● · ● · · ·

Attachment Language Translation:

Objective: Understanding each other's attachment language and finding a common tongue.

1. **Materials Needed**: Pen, paper.

2. **Instructions**:

   ○ Write down a sentence or two that your partner often says that triggers you or makes you feel insecure.

   ○ Swap papers and individually re-write the sentences using words that feel more secure and affirming.

○ Share your translations, discuss, and learn from each other's attachment language.

· · · ● · ● · ● · · ·

Emotional Check-In:

Objective: Regularly tune into each other's emotional world.

1. **Materials Needed**: A set time, like a daily or weekly date.

2. **Instructions**:

○ Share one thing that made you happy and one thing that upset you during the day or week.

○ Discuss how these events might relate to your attachment styles.

○ Offer support and understanding, even if the concerns seem small or insignificant.

· · · ● · ● · ● · · ·

The Gratitude Jar:

Objective: Cultivate appreciation and positive affirmations in your relationship.

1. **Materials Needed**: A jar, paper, and pen.

2. **Instructions**:

○ Whenever you feel appreciative of something your partner did, write it down and put it in the jar.

○ At the end of the week, sit down together and read the notes. It's like sending little love letters to each other.

The Attachment Vision Board:

Objective: Visualize and work towards a securely attached relationship.

1. **Materials Needed**: Magazines, scissors, glue, and a large piece of cardboard or paper.

2. **Instructions**:

   ○ Cut out images and words that represent your goals for your relationship.

   ○ Glue them onto the board to create a visual representation of a securely attached relationship.

   ○ Discuss your choices and how you can work towards these goals together.

There may be some bumps and turns along the way to a securely attached relationship, but with each one, there's a chance to learn, grow, and become better at navigating. The magic is in sailing through the storms with someone you love, with a map full of memories of things you've done together.

Setting Boundaries

Boundaries, both emotional and physical, serve as markers on this path, guiding the relationship through the tangles of insecurities, the underbrush of past traumas, and across the rivers of emotional expression. They help to define the "I" in the "We," making sure that while the journey is shared, the individuality is not lost.

Let's get into the details of setting boundaries, which may seem simple but actually requires a combination of self-awareness, communication, and respect.

$$\cdot \; \cdot \; \bullet \; \bullet \; \cdot \; \bullet \; \cdot \; \bullet \; \bullet \; \cdot \; \cdot$$

The Why and The How of Boundary-Setting

Self-Preservation: Setting limits is essentially a form of self-preservation. It's about knowing your limits and making sure that other people respect them. According to research, people who have clear boundaries tend to have higher self-esteem and less stress because they can effectively advocate for their needs and protect their emotional health.

Promoting Equality: Boundaries promote equality in relationships. When both people can be honest about their wants, fears, and needs, a balanced dynamic is created and neither person feels ignored or overshadowed.

Fostering Trust and Security: Trust is fostered when boundaries are respected. A secure attachment is established when one's feelings and needs are acknowledged.

Enhancing Understanding: By being clear about one's limits, one can better understand and respect the needs and limitations of the other person, which is essential to maintaining a securely attached relationship.

$$\cdot \; \cdot \; \bullet \; \bullet \; \cdot \; \bullet \; \cdot \; \bullet \; \bullet \; \cdot \; \cdot$$

Setting Boundaries - A Two-Pronged Approach

Self-Reflection: Self-reflection is the first step. Setting meaningful boundaries requires first understanding one's own needs, fears, and desires. It involves going through one's own emotional maze, figuring out what sets you off, and knowing what makes you feel good and what doesn't.

Communication: The next crucial step is to make these boundaries clear to your partner. Honesty, clarity, and assertiveness are necessary. It's important to understand and respect the boundaries that your partner has set for you as well as your own. A healthy and secure attachment relationship is based on both parties understanding and respecting each other's boundaries.

Setting limits does not mean building walls that can't be broken through. Building gates allows for the free flow of feelings, understanding, and respect while keeping out negativity, disrespect, and disregard. Through this delicate balance, relationships can flourish in the lush, open space of secure attachment, where each person can grow as themselves and as a part of the relationship.

In fact, developing a secure attachment style is a team effort rather than an individual one. It's like dancing with others to the beat of life; every step, turn, and pause is not just your own accomplishment, but a group effort. Our attachments, which are intertwined with the core of our relationships, serve as mirrors, reflecting both our own emotional landscapes and the emotional landscapes of the people we are connected to.

The dynamics of our relationships also shift along the attachment spectrum as we move closer to a more secure attachment style. Every interaction we have with our partners, friends, or family members—whether it be through conversation, shared silence, laughter, or disagreement—leaves its mark on our attachment styles.

It's a dance of growing together, of tuning our strings to fit with each other's without losing our own unique notes. As we play the chords of secure attachment, the melody echoes through the halls of our relationships, making a tune that is comforting, calming, and nurturing.

As you step onto the dance floor, remember that every step you take resonates through the dance hall of life and in the hearts and souls of those you dance with. Here's to a dance that is rhythmic, harmonious, and sprinkled with the grace of secure attachment, leading not only to a melody that stirs the soul but also to relationships that are warm and deeply satisfying.

Chapter Sixteen

Advanced Topics and Further Resources

Congratulations on making it to this point in your journey through the maze of attachment. It's not a small accomplishment; rather, it shows how dedicated you are to growing as a person and in your relationships. Now that you've gone beyond the basics of attachment theory, you can better understand how people connect with one another. The search for understanding attachment, however, is not a destination but rather a journey that never ends.

As diverse and vast as the human experience itself is the landscape of attachment. New levels of understanding, new spheres of connection, and new horizons of self-discovery are revealed with each relationship we build, interaction we have, and emotional wave we ride.

It's both an end and a beginning to be where you are right now, looking out at the vast ocean of knowledge and experiences that you have yet to discover. You have a strong vessel thanks to the chapters of insight you've read so far. There is a vast ocean of advanced topics, additional readings, and resources that are calling to you with the promise of better relationships and deeper understanding.

We'll get into some more advanced topics in the pages that follow that will help you understand the nuances of attachment theory and how it can be used in different areas of life. To satisfy your thirst for more knowledge, a list of additional resources is also available.

Let's move into the higher levels of attachment with the same spirit of exploration and openness that has led you this far, with a heart full of curiosity and a mind sharpened by understanding.

· · · ● · ● · ● · · ·

The Intersection of Attachment and Mental Health

Peeling back the layers of the complicated connections between attachment styles and mental health is like peeling an onion; each layer reveals a new level of understanding, and sometimes it makes you cry. The relationship between attachment and mental health is complex and deeply affecting, resonating through the pathways of a person's psychological well-being.

The blueprints for how we understand and react to closeness and relationship expectations, known as attachment styles, are not just internal. They coexist and interact with other aspects of our mental health. Let's delve into the maze of this interaction, shall we?

Depression, the dark cloud that hangs over people's emotions for a long time, has been linked to attachment styles. These attachment styles can create a fertile environment for depressive symptoms to take hold and grow because they frequently foster a constant fear of rejection or strong walls of emotional unavailability.

Anxiety and attachment dance on the same floor. An anxious attachment style, such as a fear of being left alone or a constant need for approval, may make anxiety disorders worse, according to research. Worrying all the time that you won't be good enough or that you'll be left on the cold plains of indifference can fuel anxiety and turn a small fire into a raging blaze.

Now, let's talk about personality disorders, which are unhealthy ways of thinking, acting, and functioning that follow a person like a shadow. The story of personality disorders is also woven into the fabric of attachment. Borderline Personality Disorder (BPD), which is marked by unstable relationships, strong emotions, and impulsivity, has been linked to disorganized attachment. The tumultuous nature of disorganized attachment, where the rules of engagement in relationships are as random as rolling dice, is frequently mirrored by the chaotic whirlpool of emotions and behaviors in BPD.

The story doesn't end here. Other mental health issues are also impacted by attachment styles. The interdependence is profound, and realizing this can help you understand yourself better and plan therapeutic interventions.

Recognizing the importance of attachment in mental well-being provides clarity and direction. Although it's a complex subject, with the right guidance, it can lead to better mental health outcomes.

A study in the journal "Attachment & Human Development" and an article from the US National Library of Medicine and the National Institutes of Health were some of the sources that helped shape this investigation. These go into great detail about the connection between attachment styles and mental health disorders, giving us a wealth of information to help us understand this complicated play.[12]

• • • ● • ● • ● • •

Polyamory and Attachment

Attachment extends beyond traditional relationships to encompass non-traditional structures, such as polyamory. In polyamorous relationships, love and intimacy are shared among multiple partners, presenting their own unique dynamics.

Polyamory, as opposed to monogamy, entails multiple romantic relationships that are carried out with the consent and knowledge of all parties involved. However, just as in monogamous relationships, the attachment styles of individuals in polyamorous relationships significantly contribute to the dynamics of these connections.

Research has found that individuals with secure attachment styles were more likely to be satisfied in their polyamorous relationships. The secure individuals felt more compersion (happiness for their partner's romantic and sexual adventures with others) and less jealousy compared to those with insecure attachment styles.[3]

But it's not just the securely attached who walk the paths of polyamory. Individuals with anxious and avoidant attachment styles also navigate the polyamorous terrain, each with their unique set of challenges and experiences. Some research suggests that individuals with an anxious attachment style might find the openness and multiple connections in polyamory to be anxiety-provoking. On the flip side, those with avoidant attachment styles might find the freedom and lack of restriction in polyamory to be appealing.[4]

However, just as a rose can thrive in the wild, insecure attachment styles can evolve in the open fields of polyamory. Individuals, regardless of their attachment style, can engage in fulfilling polyamorous relationships with awareness, communication, and a willingness to face the music of their attachment dynamics.

In the same breath, some have turned to polyamory to heal and grow. It's analogous to choosing to play in an orchestra to overcome the fear of performing solo. Polyamory allows people to explore, confront, and work through their attachment issues in a diversified setting, under different lights, and with different co-actors on the relationship stage.

So, whether it's a solitary or a group dance, the steps of attachment are learned, practiced, and refined over time. As one act concludes, the stage is set for the next, where the choreography of attachment continues to evolve in the limitless theater of relationships.

• • • ● •● • ● • ● •• •

Further Reading and Resources

In non-traditional relationships, particularly polyamory, attachment styles manifest differently. The dynamics of polyamory—maintaining multiple romantic or sexual relationships with the consent of all parties involved—inevitably influence and are influenced by individual attachment styles. Here's a more nuanced look at this intriguing interplay.

Broadening the Attachment Horizon

Polyamory is frequently viewed as a test bed for attachment theories on a larger scale. Unlike monogamous relationships, polyamory introduces a multi-faceted attachment scenario in which individuals navigate their attachment needs and fears with multiple partners. This environment has the potential to either exacerbate attachment insecurities or pave the way for attachment healing and growth.

In a study conducted by Moors, Matsick, Ziegler, Rubin, and Conley (2014)[5], it was found that individuals who identify as polyamorous tend to display secure attachment styles. According to the study, the open communication and consent-based nature of polyamorous relationships may promote a secure attachment environment. The inherent need for communication and negotiation in polyamorous relationships could be viewed as fertile ground for developing secure attachments.

The Anxious-Avoidant Trap in Polyamory

It's not always a rosy picture, though. The complexities of polyamory can also breed anxious and avoidant attachment behaviors. Particularly in situations where a person feels neglected or undervalued by their partners, having multiple relationships may increase attachment fears. An anxious attached person may find the lack of constant reassurance in polyamory to be an anxiety roller-coaster, whereas an avoidant attached person may see it as an opportunity to maintain emotional distance.

Attachment Fluidity in Polyamory

Polyamory, interestingly, could also be used as a platform for exploring and potentially changing one's attachment style. The dynamics of polyamory encourage individuals to confront and openly communicate their needs and fears with multiple partners, which may foster a deeper understanding and possibly a shift in attachment style over time.

The Echoes of Mono-normativity

The societal norm of monogamy can cast a long shadow on polyamorous relationships. Individuals in polyamorous relationships frequently navigate a society that may not fully understand or accept their relationship structure, which can have an impact on attachment dynamics. The societal pressure and potential stigma associated with polyamory may influence how secure, anxious, or avoidant attachment styles manifest in these non-traditional relationships.

The narrative of attachment within polyamory reveals a landscape rich in emotional exploration, challenges, and growth. The interaction between attachment styles and polyamory sheds light on the fluid nature of attachment, implying that non-traditional relationships may offer a unique perspective on attachment theory and a path toward fostering secure attachments.

References:

1. Moors, A. C., Matsick, J. L., Ziegler, A., Rubin, J. D., & Conley, T. D. (2014). Working Models of Attachment to Close Others and to the Relationship Script of Consensual Non-monogamy. Sexual and Relationship Therapy, 29(1), 75-91.

2. "Polyamory and Attachment Style: The Relationship Between Attachment Style and Relationship Structure in Polyamorous Relationships". (n.d.). ResearchGate.

3. "How Attachment Styles Translate To Polyamory". (n.d.). FetVancouver.com.

4. "Attachment and Polyamory: Relationship Structures and Attachment Styles among Polyamorous Individuals". (n.d.). ResearchGate.

5. "Attachment Styles and Polyamory: A Closer Look". (n.d.). Healthline.

It's time to take a breather and reflect on the vast terrain we've covered as we close the chapter on advanced topics and additional resources. From the cradle of attachment in infancy to its manifestation in the tapestry of adult relationships, the journey has been both illuminating and enriching. The interaction of attachment with mental health, as well as its dance across the spectrum of monogamous to polygamous relationships, has provided insight into the complexities and beauty of human connections.

Despite our discoveries, the field of attachment is as vast as the human experience itself. Each relationship we form, whether temporary or permanent, adds a new hue to our understanding of attachment. And as life unfolds, so does the enigmatic story of attachment, constantly weaving new threads into our evolving understanding.

As we move on to the next section, "The Journey Ahead," keep in mind that the quest to understand attachment is a lifelong adventure, not a destination. The horizon is brimming with potential for deeper connection, personal growth, and a better understanding of oneself and others. As you turn the page, may your mind remain curious, your heart open, and your spirit ever resilient on this never-ending journey of discovery.

---

1. https://traumaonline.net/courses/attachment-and-trauma-at/

2. https://mauimindfultherapy.com/neuroscience-attachment-theory/

3. https://link.springer.com/article/10.1007/s12119-021-09902-0

4. https://link.springer.com/article/10.1007/s12119-023-10120-z

5. https://digitalcommons.chapman.edu/psychology_articles/133/

CHAPTER SEVENTEEN

THE JOURNEY AHEAD

As you close this book, take a moment to thank yourself for your dedication and hard work on this journey to understand and improve your attachment style. It's no easy task to delve into the tender realms of attachment, confront the patterns that have shaped your relationships, and embark on a path of transformation.

The exploration of attachment is similar to peeling layers of an onion. Each layer reveals a deeper understanding, a more nuanced perspective of how we relate to others and ourselves. And, just as an onion can make you cry, the journey may have had some poignant moments. Nevertheless, with each layer peeled and insight gained, you have taken steps toward cultivating more secure and enriching relationships.

The pages of this book may come to an end, but your journey does not. The road ahead is paved with opportunities for development, cultivating secure attachments, and continuing to enrich your relationships. It's a rewarding and difficult path. And remember that your journey is unique in its challenges and triumphs.

You now have access to a wealth of information, exercises, and insights. As you move forward in your life, you will have the tools to continue nurturing your relationships, to delve deeper into the mysteries of attachment, and to seek professional guidance when necessary.

The tapestry of human connection is ever-evolving, and as you continue on this path, may your relationships blossom into the most beautiful patterns, woven with threads of understanding, empathy, and secure attachment. Your journey into the realms of attachment demonstrates your tenacity, desire for development, and capacity for profound connection.

So here's to you, your journey, and the beautiful horizons that await you. The journey of self-discovery and relational growth is infinite, and each day may bring you closer to the heart of secure attachment, enriching not only your life but the lives of those you love.

What You've Learned

The voyage through the realms of attachment you've undertaken has been expansive and profound. Here's a distillation of the quintessence from each chapter that now forms part of your intellectual and emotional repertoire:

1. **Understanding Attachment**: Dipped into the genesis of attachment theory, understanding its profound impact on how we relate to others.

2. **Attachment Styles**: Unveiled the four primary attachment styles, offering a mirror to see your relational dynamics more clearly.

3. **The Neuroscience of Attachment and Trauma**: Delved into how trauma can sculpt the brain's reactions, influencing attachment styles.

4. **Self-Assessment: Discover Your Attachment Style**: Invited introspection through a nuanced questionnaire, shedding light on your attachment tendencies.

5. **Parenting and Attachment: An Overview**: Explored the ripple effect of parenting on attachment, laying down the canvas for nurturing secure attachments in children.

6. **Parenting the Securely Attached Child**: Uncovered the hallmarks of secure attachment in children and how to foster such a nurturing environment.

7. **Parenting the Anxiously Attached Child**: Discussed the challenges and strategies to help anxiously attached children find their emotional equilibrium.

8. **Parenting the Avoidant Child**: Navigated through the avoidant attachment landscape in children, offering strategies for emotional engagement.

9. **Parenting the Disorganized/Fearful-Avoidant Child**: Unravelled the complex emotional threads of disorganized attachment, suggesting a path towards stability.

10. **Navigating Secure Attachment**: Touched upon the serenity and fortitude inherent in secure attachment, offering exercises to foster it.

11. **Understanding and Improving Anxious Attachment**: Ventured into the anxious mind, offering a toolkit of exercises for managing anxious attachment tendencies.

12. **The Complexities of Avoidant Attachment**: Shone light on the avoidant's emotional armor, proposing exercises for opening up.

13. **The Enigma of Disorganized/Fearful-Avoidant Attachment**: Dissected the disorganized attachment style, offering strategies for achieving emotional stability.

14. **Exercises That Aren't Dull as Dishwater**: Spiced up the journey with engaging exercises aimed at illuminating and improving your attachment style.

15. **How to Work on Your Attachment Style in Relationships**: Unveiled the dynamics of working on attachment issues within the relational arena, offering exercises for couples.

16. **Advanced Topics and Further Resources**: Broached advanced topics like the intersection of mental health and attachment, and polyamory.

17. **The Journey Ahead**: Reiterated the continuous nature of this journey, urging you to keep exploring, learning, and growing in the realm of attachment.

Final Words

We are at the crossroads of newfound understanding and the prospect of richer, more secure relationships. This book aimed to untangle the delicate web of attachment, giving you the lens to see yourself and your relationships more clearly. However, the pages of this book only scratch the surface of a profound and personal journey toward self-awareness and relational fulfillment.

The path to understanding and improving one's attachment style isn't always clear; it's a winding path with its fair share of thorns and blossoms. It's an adventure filled with self-reflection, open conversations, and the courage to delve into the emotional caverns that frequently hold the keys to our relationship patterns.

But despite the difficulties, this journey holds the powerful promise of transformation. A promise of nurturing, secure, and satisfying relationships. A promise of developing into a version of oneself that is more sensitive to the emotional landscapes within and around us.

Every step you take on this path, whether it's self-reflection, therapy, or simply being more mindful in your interactions, is a step toward a more secure attachment style. It's a step toward relationships marked by mutual understanding, trust, and a strong bond that endures the test of time.

As you continue on this journey, remember that the essence of this journey lies in the process itself—the insights gained, the old patterns shed, and the new, healthier patterns embraced. It's about celebrating your incremental progress and cherishing the evolving narrative of your relationship life.

As you close this book, may you carry with you the curiosity to investigate, the courage to confront the shadows, and the hope of nurturing relationships that are as fulfilling as they are secure. Your journey through the realms of attachment is a testament to your tenacity and unwavering pursuit of emotional growth and fulfilling connections.

Here's to the journey ahead, the discoveries it holds, and the beautiful, intricate, and ever-evolving tapestry of human connection.

Appendices

Appendix A: Additional Resources

1. **Books:**

   - "Attached" by Amir Levine and Rachel Heller

   - "Hold Me Tight" by Dr. Sue Johnson

   - "The Body Keeps the Score" by Bessel van der Kolk

2. **Websites:**

   - The Gottman Institute (www.gottman.com)

   - Psychology Today's Attachment Theory page (www.psychologytoday.com)

3. **Podcasts:**

   - "The Attachment Theory Podcast"

   - "Where Should We Begin?" with Esther Perel

4. **Online Therapy Platforms:**

   - BetterHelp (www.betterhelp.com)

   - TalkSpace (www.talkspace.com)

Appendix B: Glossary

- **Attachment:** A deep emotional bond between two individuals.

- **Attachment Style:** The way in which an individual relates to others, often rooted in early childhood experiences.

- **Anxious Attachment:** An attachment style characterized by a strong fear of abandonment.

- **Avoidant Attachment:** An attachment style characterized by a desire for independence and emotional distance.

- **Secure Attachment:** An attachment style characterized by comfort with closeness and independence.

- **Disorganized Attachment:** An attachment style characterized by confusion and a lack of clear attachment behavior.

PLEASE CONSIDER LEAVING A REVIEW

Hello there!

As an author, I know just how important reviews are for getting the word out about my work. When readers leave a review on Amazon or any other book stores, it helps others discover my book and decide whether it's right for them.

Plus, it gives me valuable feedback on what readers enjoyed and what they didn't.

So if you've read my book and enjoyed it (or even if you didn't!), I would really appreciate it if you took a moment to leave a review on Amazon. It doesn't have to be long or complicated - just a few words about what you thought of the book would be incredibly helpful.

Thank you so much for your support!

Jeff

. . . ● . ● . ● . . .

Adulting Hard for Young Women

. . . ● . ● . ● . . .

Adulting Hard After College

. . . ● . ● . ● . . .

Adulting Hard in Your Late Twenties and Thirties

Adulting Hard For Couples

Adulting Hard for New Parents

• • • ● • ● • ● • • •

Adulting Hard as an Introvert or Highly Sensitive Person

• • • ● • ● • ● • • •

Adulting Hard and Laughing Harder

• • • ● • ● • ● • • •

101 Questions to Ask Before You Get Engaged